THE
SPIRITUAL ESPOUSALS

BLESSED JAN VAN RUYSBROEK

THE SPIRITUAL ESPOUSALS

translated from the Dutch
with an introduction by

ERIC COLLEDGE

CHRISTIAN CLASSICS
P.O. Box 30
Westminster, Maryland 21157

First Published In English, 1953
Reprinted 1983

Library Of Congress Catalog Card Number: 83-071389
ISBN 0-87061-078-3
Printed In USA

To
CHARLES MULCAHY

CONTENTS

TRANSLATOR'S NOTE

My translation of *The Spiritual Espousals* has been made from the text to be found in Vol. I of *Werken* (for fuller information concerning this and other works cited in the Introduction, see the Bibliography), the critical edition of all Ruysbroek's works published to mark the 550th anniversary of his death. I have followed this excellent edition in most cases in its punctuation and paragraphing, and I have also translated its modern Dutch chapter-titles, which, although they do not seem to be Ruysbroek's own, derive from several of the best medieval Dutch and Latin manuscripts.

I have incurred debts to many scholars, and first I should acknowledge the work of two anonymous Englishmen of the 15th century, probably both Carthusians, the translator of *The Treatise of Perfection of the Sons of God* and the author-compiler of *The Chastising of God's Children*, much of which second work is taken direct from some Latin version of the *Espousals*. It was they who first introduced me to Ruysbroek, and showed me how well he repays a translator's pains.

Among the living, I have to thank Monsignor R. A. Knox, the Rev. Michael Egan, S.J., and the Rev. Vincent Wilkin, S.J., all of whom have given me valuable counsel. My colleague Professor E. Allison Peers, the general editor of this series, has put all his great knowledge and experience most generously at my disposal. And the labours and dilemmas inseparable from the preparation of such a book as this have been lessened for me by my mother's expert help and sound advice.

JAN VAN RUYSBROEK

born in South Brabant 1293
ordained priest c. 1317
retired from secular life 1343
professed as Augustinian 1351
died 2 December 1381
beatified 1908

INTRODUCTION

FEW writers, even among the saints, have told us as little of themselves as Blessed Jan van Ruysbroek. Everything that he wrote, and he was a copious writer, conveys to us a warm, lively, arresting personality; but he is at scrupulous pains to avoid telling us who or what he was. Still more, he is at pains not to claim for himself any merit or pre-eminence as a contemplative. His books are all works of instruction in the contemplative life, and he is never tired of insisting that this life can be achieved only if man seek God Himself alone, and not in or through His creatures; and this is given practical application in his writings, in which he is plainly concerned not to offer, to those who seek guidance from them, any of the distractions or hindrances to enlightenment which a display of his personality might afford.

The circle of devoted friends which grew around him in his own priory of Groenendael outside Brussels, and in other religious houses of the Low Countries, produced several biographers whose records enable us to measure the difference between the impression which his treatises give, not, it is true, of frigidity or inhumanity, but of withdrawal, and the seductive powers of his conversation and manners. But nothing which these biographers have written suggests the intractability or the contentiousness which are too often the marks of the controversial theologian. His life, as well as his works, was marked by a humility and a serenity which must have cost much to achieve and maintain; for his writings make it plain that in his own lifetime, as thereafter, he was attacked as a teacher of false doctrine.

The Church of which he lived and died a faithful son, in beatifying him, gave at last her guarantee that he did not teach heresy; but it is not uncommon, even today, to find the old

9

charges resurrected, that Ruysbroek held views and employed language which are almost indistinguishable from those of Pantheists and Quietists. Such charges are usually reinforced by quotations from *The Spiritual Espousals*.

If we are to interpret the *Espousals* in the sense which Ruysbroek intended, and if we are not similarly to misunderstand and calumniate him, we must know more of him and of the times for which he wrote than can be learned from his works. It is true that there is a vital relationship between his doctrine and the heresies of which he has been accused; but this relationship is that of the completed picture to the scattered, disjointed, meaningless and misleading fragments of a jigsaw puzzle. *In minimis*, Ruysbroek's doctrine reflects a principle very often to be observed in the history of Christianity, that it is the perversions of truth which call forth the ultimate and authoritative definition of truth.

Ruysbroek, who was born in 1293, had already spent many years in Brussels as a secular priest, serving the collegiate church of St. Gudule in a humble office, and devoting himself to prayer, contemplation, study and the cure of souls, when, some years before 1344 (no exact date is possible), he first became prominent, and that through the vigorous part he took in attacking the heretical doctrines which had been spread by the female apostle of 'seraphic love', Bloemardinne.[1] She is a somewhat ambiguous figure among the many heretics, male and female, who flourished in the Low Countries towards the close of the Middle Ages, but we have some evidence on which to base our conjectures as to the exact nature of the doctrines Ruysbroek felt himself called to denounce.[2] It is however significant that, as is so often the case with such

[1] The details of Ruysbroek's life given here are principally derived from the second essay of D. A. Stracke, S.J., chapter iv of *Leven* (see the Bibliography for this and other full titles): and in this essay will also be found an excellent critical examination of the sources for the Ruysbroek biographical writings.

[2] J. Van Mierlo, S.J., has contributed two articles, 'Bégardisme' and 'Bloemardinne', to the *Dictionnaire d'histoire et de géographie ecclésiastiques*, to which I am much indebted for the account here, as to Mgr. Knox's *Enthusiasm*, which I shall have frequent occasion to quote.

heretical movements, no contemporary documents survive, although Pomerius, the Groenendael Augustinian who compiled the first authoritative biography of Ruysbroek, writing in the second decade of the fifteenth century, says that he has seen her books himself and can testify to their pernicious nature. Furthermore, we have no work of Ruysbroek which manifestly is the immediate outcome of his campaign against her: Stracke suggests that probably he confined himself to preaching to combat her influence, which had become so great as to be an open scandal in Brussels; but if Stracke's conjecture is correct, a further reason may well be that Ruysbroek saw the dangers that could attend a documentation of her beliefs which might gain circulation and so vitiate the success which, it would seem, his mission enjoyed.

Pomerius, who is thus our principal source of knowledge of Bloemardinne, tells us that she taught and wrote of 'the liberty of the spirit' and of 'the seraphic nature of free love'; for the rest, he merely describes the fame and powerful patronage she enjoyed in life, and the veneration accorded her after her death, which seems to have taken place before Ruysbroek began his campaign.

Before we leave Pomerius' account of her, however, we must notice one somewhat curious statement in it which has given rise to much controversy. He identifies Bloemardinne with her near-contemporary, the mysterious 'Hadewijch', of whom we know almost nothing except that she was the author of numerous poems, celebrating her adoration of the Redeemer, and often couched in the language of courtly love. This conflation, as he regards it, is absolutely rejected by Van Mierlo; and the curious reader must be referred to his article for the details of his highly ingenious theory that Pomerius, officially deputed to scrutinize Hadewijch's verses, was unable to distinguish between her use of erotic imagery to convey sentiments in themselves unexceptionable, and Bloemardinne's celebrations of 'seraphic love'. There is no need to make this discussion of Ruysbroek's writings unduly involved, or to relate Van Mierlo's thesis to that other, made prominent in recent years by M. Denis de Rougemont, which identifies the imagery of the poetry of courtly love with the symbolism of Cathar heresy; but it is relevant to present considerations to remark here that although Ruysbroek was perfectly familiar with the symbol, so often used, of Christ as the knightly champion and wooer of the soul, he hardly ever employs it in the *Espousals*, where it would have been most appropriate (the most obvious reflections of such symbolism are the phrases 'He dies well who dies for love'—II xi 4—and 'He has laboured and striven as a champion against our foes'— Prologue); and, further, although he does in fact in *The Twelve Beguines* quote and acknowledge some quite harmless verses by Hadewijch (this is one of Van Mierlo's chief reasons for rejecting the identification with Bloemardinne), he himself is never to be found employing erotic imagery. In the *Espousals*, the principal suggestion of such imagery is in his simile of the bee that ravishes the flower (II x 5); and even that would not be distasteful, were it not for the association which it suggests with many outpourings of ecstatic mystics, usually women, which are not always edifying.

Had Willem Jordaens, Ruysbroek's confrère and disciple, observed a similar discretion in his Latin translation of the *Espousals*, the earliest which has survived, although Geert Groote composed another, now lost, much harm might have been avoided. Unfortunately, all is zeal. He was so anxious to win approbation for his master, and to make plain his dark sayings, that his *De Ornatu* begins with a prologue which most scholars agree to regard as a pious forgery,[1] and the ensuing translation contains much which is not faithful and accurate translation, and some matter which woefully misrepresents the original. One example will suffice, from the first sentence of Book III: where Ruysbroek writes ' . . . soe comt die innighe mensche in een godscouwende leven', Jordaens has thought

---

[1] I am aware of the theory, put forward in our own times, that Ruysbroek himself was the author of both prologue and translation; but my own collation of Jordaens' Latin and Ruysbroek's Dutch has satisfied me that this hypothesis can be disregarded.

fit to render this as 'introducitur amator devotus velut in sponsi cubiculum in vitam contemplativam'. Instances can be multiplied of such use of thought and language quite alien from Ruysbroek's own; and Jordaens must bear a part of the responsibility for the grave scandal and offence which his translation caused to Jean Gerson, Chancellor of Paris University in the early fifteenth century, who was moved to write an attack on Ruysbroek as a teacher of heresy.

Not all the blame attaches to Jordaens. Schoonhoven, the Groenendael canon who undertook the defence of Ruysbroek's reputation against Gerson's attacks, and, following Schoonhoven, Gerhardt Hamont, the prior of the Cologne Charterhouse who wrote the preface to the new Latin translation by Laurenz Surius, his confrère, and who makes it clear that this translation was undertaken to remove the false impressions created by Jordaens' work, seek to apportion fairly this blame: it is impossible to judge Ruysbroek solely on Jordaens' showing, impossible to judge the *Espousals* solely on Book III, as Gerson seems to do, and impossible to understand the *Espousals* for what it is without reference to the whole body of Ruysbroek's writings.

We have evidence to show that Ruysbroek himself was well aware that his works might be misinterpreted as advancing Pantheist and Quietist opinions, and also that he foresaw the dangers that might arise from a too wide circulation of the earlier books, which he had not intended for general reading. We know this from the prologue by the Herne Carthusian, Gheraert van Saintes, to the manuscript written in Herne Charterhouse to contain a collection of five of the principal treatises, beginning with *The Kingdom of Lovers*, continuing with the *Espousals*, and ending with *The Little Book of Enlightenment*. Gheraert describes how he and some of his brethren asked Ruysbroek to visit them at Herne to expound his doctrine, which they had failed to understand perfectly from his writings. He came to them, and in private conversation Gheraert asked for his own explanation of certain passages in the *Kingdom*. Ruysbroek was perturbed to know that this work had come into their hands, and 'he was sorry that the book had come into circulation (gheopenbaert was), for it was the first book that he had made, and a priest who had been Sir Jan's secretary, whom he had forbidden to publish it (voirtsetten), had secretly lent it to us to copy'. Gheraert then offered to surrender their copy to Ruysbroek, but he refused this, saying that he would instead write a work of explanation of the terms employed in his early works, and of how he intended men to understand them.[1]

The promised work is *The Little Book of Enlightenment*, and in his prologue to it Ruysbroek confirms Gheraert van Saintes' account: 'Some of my friends wish me and have asked me with short words to expound and make plain as well as I am able the nearest and the clearest truth which I understand and feel concerning all the most exalted doctrines of which I have written, so that no-one should be angered by them, but that everyone be improved.'[2] Ruysbroek is probably poking fun at himself here for his verbosity and his love of polysyllabic abstract nouns; and in the *Little Book* he does with a will what he has been asked. Although it is a misrepresentation to call it, as Pomerius did, a 'retractio', for its essence is that its author has nothing to withdraw, since he has never held heretical views, it is, none the less, a denunciation of Pantheism and Quietism forthright and vehement, and had Gerson and his many followers ever known of it, they could not have remained in doubt about the true interpretation of the *Espousals*.

In my account of Ruysbroek's system, I shall quote chiefly, where quotation helps to clarify, from the *Little Book* and from *The Twelve Beguines*: these are both late works, written in an awareness of hostile critics, and intended primarily for readers not far advanced in contemplation, and therefore in need of aids to the study of the more difficult works, such as *The Spiritual Tabernacle*, the *Kingdom* and the *Espousals*.

But in thus contrasting works for beginners with works for more advanced students, we must not fall into the error of

[1] *Werken* III lxii–iii.
[2] *Werken* III 276.

supposing that there is any fundamental discrepancy between the two categories. The *Espousals* is only capable of mis-interpretation because it is, judged solely on the intellectual level, a superb readjustment, reassessment and reformation of the truths of which Pantheism and Quietism are a distortion; and in the *Espousals* there is an almost complete absence of negative condemnation of these distortions, because Ruysbroek believed that in combating them his most powerful weapon was affirmation of Divine truth as it was revealed to him. In this affirmation, he proceeds far beyond the local and particular controversies of his own day to a recognition of the spiritual and intellectual defects which will lead in any age to heresy and schism; and he sees clearly that heretics and schismatics have no monopoly of such defects.

Consider from this point of view his examination of the effects of the theological virtues upon conduct (I xix–xxix). The humble man is free from dissimulation and affectation: the obedient man is submissive to Holy Church and her prelates and ordinances: the self-denying man will not seek to be different from the saints: the patient man will suffer quietly under oppression and persecution: the meek man is able to endure harsh words and treatment: the merciful man will return love for anger: the compassionate man will be moved by the sufferings of all humanity: the mild man, contemplating the errors of humanity, will be drawn the more to God against Whom humanity sins: the sober man will neither taste nor know forbidden things.

This repertory, with its careful and ingenious relation of each item to the Beatitudes and to the deadly sins, a wonderful example in itself of the skill of the medieval rhetorician, is also a percipient catalogue of the excesses into which pride, disobedience, anger and the rest have led, and still lead, distracted humanity; and in its recognition of human society for what it is when it forgoes the grace of God, it is as much removed from the Quietism of his day as from the belief so prevalent now that society can somehow render itself innocuous without superior aid.

This does not, however, imply that Ruysbroek was incapable of applying the method of the *Espousals* to the specific ills of his own times. He was too well aware of them to wish to avoid them; and he shows himself to be particularly conscious of the special dangers that accompany the pursuit of the contemplative life. We may in this connexion contrast his description of the eccentric conduct of those visited with 'spiritual drunkenness' (II x 3) with what he writes of the psychological state of the 'tempestuous man' (II xi 4). Although there is perhaps some irony, even at his own expense, in his treatment of 'spiritual drunkards', he is not led by their extravagant behaviour to impute to them any fault or error, however much the world may disapprove; but he is stern in his warnings to tempestuous men against the wish for death which will visit them. It is evident that he knew well how close to the God-given mystical rapture can come a morbidity in which the devil works. (It is noteworthy how often, as in this passage, he uses the figure of the 'high road', the 'main path', the route already mapped out for the contemplative, to stray from which is perilous to the soul).

We have not the evidence necessary to show us what order Ruysbroek's own perception of the truths fundamental in his system followed: a case might be made for the hypothesis that it was his recognition of the exact nature of the extravagances of Bloemardinne and her followers which led to his seeing the straight path of contemplation from which they had strayed. It is however more probable, and this is the view to which Pomerius and the other early biographers incline, that he was moved to teach against her because already his own mind was clear and illumined as concerns the verities which she was so greatly obscuring and perverting.

Knox points out, referring to an earlier advocacy of 'liberty of the spirit' than that attributed by Pomerius to Bloemardinne, that the expression has an ominous ring. We who today use such expressions as vague equivalents of 'freedom of thought' must not fall into the error of supposing that Bloemardinne was pleading for any kind of religious or intellectual tolerance:

such a plea would indeed have made her remarkable among medieval Europeans, orthodox or heretics. Her 'liberty of the spirit' is a very different doctrine, that of the liberty of spirit from flesh. Let the flesh do what it will, let its appetites be gratified, the more the better, that it may trouble less the spirit. God gave us our spirits, but they dwell in flesh which the Prince of Darkness made, and we must in this life serve two masters. So let the spirit be free to serve God, and the flesh free to serve the devil. This, then, is 'seraphic love': the angels have no flesh, and let us love as the angels love, knowing and caring as little as they what our flesh may do meanwhile. This view of human nature, pre-Christian, non-Christian and essentially anti-Christian, we usually know under the name of Dualism, and associate with the Manichean heresy. Ruysbroek's recognition of the utter incompatibility of Dualism and Christianity is given a positive expression in his own presentation of Christian doctrine concerning human nature; and unless we recognize his teaching on this point, we cannot possibly understand how opposed is his doctrine of humanity's union with God to Quietism, his doctrine of humanity's likeness to God to Pantheism.

The opening paragraphs of the *Espousals* give us the key to the interpretation of the whole book and to all Ruysbroek's works. Nature is the bride of God, and He made her in His own image: this is to be interpreted unequivocally, and beside it no Dualistic theory of the origin of matter can exist. In Mary's part in the Incarnation, God's prime intention for human nature, union with Him, is made manifest: no Docetic account of Christ's humanity can be reconciled with this; and he pursues this matter later, showing us that even though through the Fall human nature was accursed and rejected, still Christ was willing to take upon Him that nature (I ix), and showed His reverence for that nature in His miracles of healing, which, Ruysbroek significantly insists, are to be interpreted literally as well as figuratively (I x). It is this teaching on which he insists again in *The Twelve Beguines*, where he writes: 'We are all one life in God, in our everlasting image, above our created

17

being. We are also one humanity, which God has created, and we are one human nature, in which God has imprinted His image in Trinity, and which He in love took upon Himself, so that He with us is God and man. And all men have received this alike, bad and good; for this is the excellence and exaltedness of our nature, and by means of it we are neither holy nor blessed.'[1]

This is the doctrine which St. Paul explicitly states for us: 'Christ has risen from the dead, the first fruits of all those who have fallen asleep; a man had brought us death, and a man should bring us resurrection from the dead; just as all have died with Adam, so with Christ all will be brought to life.'[2]

I should like here to refer to Knox's vivacious demonstration, in his chapter entitled 'The Corinthians' Letter to St. Paul',[3] that the First Epistle to the Corinthians is in fact an itemized condemnation of the appearance in the Church of Corinth of a variety of heretical and schismatic tendencies which historians have only recognized as such as they appear later in the Church's history. From this demonstration Knox excludes the fifteenth chapter, dealing with the Resurrection; but it may well be that St. Paul's thought and language here are aimed at the beginnings of a Corinthian Dualism, and at a denial that Christ clothed Himself in our flesh and nature, for he is attacking the statements of some members of the Church that 'the dead do not rise again'. The implication of this is that they had anticipated Docetism, which taught, as Knox defines it, that Christ 'was not really born of the Virgin, and did not really die on the Cross, but wore through life a phantom body in which matter had no part'.

From Ruysbroek's affirmation that we are made in the likeness of God there proceed his views concerning the nature in us of that Divine likeness, and how likeness to God brings unity with Him.

This complex question of 'unity' is not dealt with, except superficially, in Book I, for that would not accord with

[1] *Werken* IV 30.   [2] I Corinthians xv 20–23.
[3] *Enthusiasm* cap. II.

18

Ruysbroek's careful planning of the work so that the three books correspond not merely with three stages of progress in contemplation, but also with three ascending grades of spiritual and intellectual attainment in the readers for whom it is intended. Thus in Book I, The Active Life, there is neither thought nor terminology beyond the grasp of the plain man, and a discussion there of the nature of unity would be inappropriate; but at the very beginning of Book II, The Life of Yearning, we are told that Christ showed us the way to unity, by His death in the bond of love, and by His Ascension (II i).

Following immediately upon this (II ii–iv) comes the exposition of man's 'threefold unity, natural and supernatural'. The connexion between this and the preceding statement that Christ showed us the way to unity is not at once apparent: but it is derived from the doctrines, which we have already examined, that humanity is imprinted with God's image in Trinity, and that our bearing of that image is perfectly exemplified in Christ. In its turn, this doctrine of the triune nature in man of the Divine image is derived from the view (a view on the whole Thomist and anti-Scotist, though Ruysbroek avoids any indication that the question is controversial) of the essential nature of humanity.

According to this view, man consists of body, soul and personality. So man was created by God, and so man possesses threefold unity, unity of the 'lower' or physical powers of the body, with the 'higher' or spiritual powers of the soul, in the personality. All men, good and bad, naturally possess this unity: in our lower powers we are sensual and animal, in our higher powers we are rational and spiritual, and in our personality, in which lower and higher powers are united, we are created and preserved by God in our essence. Good men further possess a like unity supernaturally: in their lower powers, through the imitation of Christ and His saints in virtue and suffering: in their higher powers, in faith, hope and love, through God's graces and gifts; and in their personality, where they have a unity with God essential but beyond comprehension, and rest in God beyond all creation. And this unity with God of the personality is 'without means', whereas virtue and suffering, faith, hope and love are 'means'.

We are to understand this term 'means' in its accepted philosophic sense. God's means to us are His grace and gifts, through which we have union with Him, as through the exercise of our means to Him, which are virtues and exercises of devotion. This union 'with means' promotes the exercise of virtues. We also have union with Him without means, 'above all gifts', and this union without means brings rest in God (II xxiv–xxvi).

This threefold natural and supernatural unity in man informs the whole of his teaching. Sensual and animal man, in the right use of his lower powers, pursues the active life of virtue and suffering, the subject-matter of Book I: rational and spiritual man, in the exercise of his higher powers, follows the yearning life of which he treats in Book II; and in Book III he shows how in the life of contemplation of our creation and preservation by God we achieve an essential, incomprehensible unity with Him and a rest in Him.

But though it is in the life of contemplation that this essential unity is achieved, it cannot be too strongly emphasized that Ruysbroek's conception is one of unity of body, soul and personality, of the active, yearning and contemplative lives. Never, in the *Espousals* or elsewhere, does he encourage us to suppose that in achieving the contemplative life, man is to abandon the active or yearning lives. Still less are we justified in thinking that the soul and personality will be freed of the body, here or in eternity. 'So with Christ all will be brought to life': to life as He has it in grace and in glory, in His Personality, Spirituality and Humanity. Ruysbroek's view of the contemplative life and of union with God is then at once the antithesis and the corrective of the Dualist theory of a necessary divorce between soul and body.

The first sentence of Book III makes plain what Ruysbroek conceives the contemplative life to be. The fervent lover of God possesses God, and himself (that is, his spiritual powers), and his life (that is, his sensual powers): God in delectable rest, his spiritual powers in love, his sensual powers in virtue; God in rest in the life of contemplation, in which his personality is exercised, his spiritual powers in love in the life of yearning, in which his spirituality is exercised, and, in the exercise of his humanity, his sensual powers in virtue in the active life.

Later in Book II, in cap. xvii, section 4, the argument demonstrates how he conceives this threefold unity of humanity and of the contemplative life to reflect the nature and being of Christ, and to be exercised in Him. In the Eucharist, Christ gives Himself in threefold manner: corporeally, in His glorified flesh and blood, spiritually, in His higher powers, and in personality, which exalts His spirituality into delectable unity with the Godhead. Our response, in receiving Him, is threefold: our lower powers are stirred to devotion to His Passion (and Ruysbroek here mentions stigmatization, as the most sublime token of such devotion of our lower powers), our higher powers in unity and charity, and our personality in eternal rest and delectation in the Godhead. Our threefold response is of threefold gratification to Christ, in the lowest, physical part of His Humanity, in His Spirit and in His Personality.

And our threefold response to Christ's threefold gift of Himself is the pattern of the threefold life, active, yearning and contemplative, no one part of which can be perfect without the others. At the opening of Book III I have translated Ruysbroek as writing that the fervent lover of God possesses God, himself and his life in 'justness and due proportion'. I have thus interpreted Ruysbroek's 'met gherechticheiden', here and in some ten other contexts, notably in the introduction to Book II, in I xviii, xxviii, II xiii and xxxviii. Similarly, in II xxxviii and the introduction to Book III I have paraphrased the adjective 'gherechte' as 'who has achieved this just and due proportion'. In all these cases I have thought such a paraphrase necessary, because merely to translate 'gherechticheit' as 'righteousness' or 'justice' would misrepresent the thought. In this respect Jordaens' Latin is superior to that of Surius, who is satisfied at the opening of Book III with 'cum justitia', whereas Jordaens writes 'cum justitia directiva'. But if we examine the passages I have now indicated, we shall see that Ruysbroek conceives this justness and its directive powers to consist in a balance and proportion, the same balance and proportion as he observes present in Christ in His Divinity and Humanity, and reflected in man in contemplation. Sometimes, it is true, he uses 'gherechticheit' in a more general sense, as when he speaks of Christ as 'the Sun of Righteousness', or of justice as the necessary attribute of the judge (I xv). But although I have, except where I have indicated, translated the noun as 'righteousness' or 'justice', and the corresponding adjective as 'righteous' or 'just', it will very often be found that the context states or implies the idea of balance and proportion. The difficulty which I have tried to solve in this way is typical of those which must attend the interpretation of a writer who uses words sometimes in a sense commonly accepted and understood, and at other times in a specialized and personal sense which their context does not always reveal.

The measure, the proportion and the simultaneity of our threefold way of life and threefold unity with God must be remembered, if we are to understand Ruysbroek's essentially dynamic conception of our unity with God, a unity which he calls 'living and fruitful' (II xviii). Out of the unity in which God dwells, He flows to His creatures, and flows back again into Himself: He flows to them in gifts and graces, and He requires the same in- and outflowing, both of His gifts and graces and of the human soul; and it is love which causes this flowing, God's love for His creatures, and His demand of their love for Him.

The terms 'flowing', 'going', are not terms which Ruysbroek finds it necessary to expound, and he seems in them to have found the perfect image to convey his conception of dynamism. God is 'an ebbing and flowing sea' (II xvii 2), and farther on he expounds the doctrine of Trinity in the same terms of the love of every Person flowing out to the other Persons. We too must flow and go, in and out, if we are to meet the Bridegroom, if we are to reflect the Divine nature of which we bear the image. We are to go out in love towards God, towards ourselves and towards our fellow-Christians (I xviii), and the going out demands a return, a flowing back, for we go out in love, love is born of the union of God and man, and love remains eternally in God. The gifts of God flow into the soul, and this flowing demands of us both that we too flow out in love, and that we flow back again into unity with God; and in the flowing back again we must return His gifts to Him, multiplied far beyond what we are capable of giving (II 8), and so there is a *perpetuum mobile* like the ebbing and flowing of the sea to which God has been compared.

The *perpetuum mobile* is well described for us in *The Twelve Beguines*, where we read: 'But between us and God the uniting evermore and ceaselessly renews itself. For the Spirit of God is flowing out and returning within. And the Spirit touches and stirs our spirit; and He demands that we live according to God's dearest will, and demands that we love God according to His excellence. This touching, which is a mean between us and God, beyond this we cannot attain. What in its depths this touching may be, and what in itself may be love, of this we can know nothing. And when we have exhausted ourselves by our works, then we begin again; for the gifts of God do not permit us to be idle.'[1]

These gifts and graces which so perpetually stir us Ruysbroek likens to streams, flowing from the inexhaustible well which is God's love for us (cf. II xviii). The first stream of grace endows man with unity of the spirit: and this unity is characterized by stability and independence of self and of others. This independence will be marked by man's turning inward, and dismissing from his memory all sensual images; and thus he achieves both natural unity, which he has by his creation, and supernatural unity, which he has by grace. This supernatural unity in its turn will incline him towards unity with God in Trinity, and thus he will live in the spirit, above sense and sensuality and with no need of corporeal revelation, which is appropriate to natural, sensual man (II xv).

At this point we must consider Ruysbroek's view of the

[1] *Werken* IV 32.

nature and function of 'image' and 'likeness', a view which is inseparable from what we have already seen of his doctrine of the threefold way of life. As it stands, the chapter which I have just summarized suggests that man in attaining to the life of yearning has passed beyond any need whatever of image and likeness; and it would be easy to associate this with the many passages in which he speaks of the need of sensual man in the active life for image and likeness (as in II xi 3, where he indicates, as a progressive order of 'true revelation', first the corporeal image which strikes sensual man in his imagination, second the comprehensible truth seized by spiritual man in his understanding, and finally rapture, which is beyond self), and from this juxtaposition to draw an analogy with, say, the Quietist aversion from meditating even upon Christ's humanity and sufferings, or the heretical Begards' doctrine that the exercise of virtues is the work of imperfect men, for the perfect soul is free of virtues.

Such an analogy would be utterly false, as we can see by reference to the passage already examined concerning the Eucharist. Its falseness will also be seen if we scrutinize Ruysbroek's teaching concerning image and likeness in the light of what we already know.

Man is made in the likeness of God, and if we lose His likeness we shall be damned (II xxiv), for likeness to Him is required of us by God (II viii). This likeness comes to us through His grace and gifts (II xxv), which are means; and God's means to us and ours to Him will cause this likeness always to increase (II xxviii). It is in this likeness that the life of spiritual man consists (II xxviii). The loving spirit, however, seeks rest in God 'above likeness' (II xxv): the time will come when it has progressed so far that it will wish to abandon likeness with all other means, graces and gifts, so that it may find, not His likeness, but Him Whom it loves (II xxxi). When in unity the soul finds Him, its likeness to Him will sink and die in Him (II xxxiii).

But, if we replace this last excerpt in its context, we find that Ruysbroek there says that in unity the soul's likeness to

God will sink and die in Him, yet in the active life, in grace, we shall always retain that likeness. 'Likeness' and 'above likeness' are not antipathetic, but complementary. He makes this plain when he writes 'For in the same instant and time, love is active, and rests in her Beloved' (II xxxiii); and again 'God comes ceaselessly into us through means (that is, in likeness) and without means (that is, above likeness), and He demands from us delectation and works, and demands that the one be always unimpeded by the other' (II xxxviii). The justness and due proportion of the contemplative life consists in the abandonment, in our personality, of likeness, and the retention and exercise of likeness in our spirituality and humanity. This same concept is stated in another form where he writes that no man can achieve rest who has not loved in yearning and action: and yearning and action must both precede and succeed rest (II xxxvii).

This truth is stated more simply for beginners in *The Twelve Beguines*, where we find: 'But if we wish to be received and chosen into the everlasting joy of God, we must be clothed with the life of Our Lord Jesus Christ, and united to Him in ourselves by means of His grace and our good works. And so He lives in us and we in Him, according to the measure of His grace and our holy living. And we must also be one with God above ourselves in love and in delectation. And thus we are one with Him; and thus we are one love and one delectation with Him, transfused with everlasting blessedness. And between likeness in ourselves and unity in God, the mean is the living spark of our souls, that is, the light and fire of the Holy Spirit. The light shows us that we are one with God in love and in delectation, and like to Him by means of His grace and our virtue'.[1] And in *The Little Book* we read: 'And thus must (the contemplative) go out, living, in virtues, and go in, dying, in God. And in these two is set a perfect life; and these two are as closely united as are matter and form, as are soul and body.'[2]

What is true of 'likeness' is equally true of 'images',

---

[1] *Werken* IV 34-5.   [2] *Werken* III 282-3.

although we must here observe a further caution, and distinguish between what Ruysbroek writes of images of God, and what he teaches us of images of God's creatures. Both sorts of image are means which operate upon our sensual nature, but we must use them variously. The image of God will lead us to Him, and in the active life the devout man may imagine Him under whatever name he pleases, and it shall be pleasing to Him; but, in being led to Him, in the yearning life man is distracted by the image of His creatures. In the introduction to Book II, we are told that if man is to see supernaturally, the second condition is that he must be free of 'alien images'. This is a parallel with the beginning of Book I, in which the conditions for natural, physical sight are described, and the exact correspondence is with the third condition described there, that the eyes themselves be keen and healthy. The imagination of God's creatures is treated as a kind of spiritual blindness; and we may compare this with the passage in which we are told that whereas God works from within, outward, through grace, creatures work from without, inward, through fantasies and sensual images (II vi). These images may be of the joys or the sorrows which our love of the created world may bring us (II vii): whichever they be, they are burdens which we must throw off.

But so far as the images of God are concerned, as in the case of likeness to Him, we must learn at once to use them and abandon them. That this and nothing else is Ruysbroek's meaning is made very plain if we place his words concerning our 'passing beyond' Christ's created humanity in their immediate context (II xvii 4), where he says that by the aid of His personality we must pass beyond ourselves and His humanity and rest in the Godhead, and then goes on at once to say that we achieve this by the exercise of our spirituality and the reception of grace, and by the exercise of our humanity in devotion. He no more means by this that we should in our active and yearning lives ignore Christ's humanity and Spirit than he means that in attaining to contemplation we should cease to practise virtue and to acquire grace.

How far this would be from his entire way of thought and devotion we can measure by remarking the extreme caution he uses in elaborating the Pauline figure of 'dying into life'. The figure itself, as employed by St. Paul, whom he so deeply reverenced and understood, he uses without fear: 'In the beginning (that is, in *The Kingdom*) I have said thus, that all good men are united with God through means. This means is the grace of God and the sacraments of Holy Church and godly virtues: faith, hope and love, and a virtuous life according to the commandments of God. And to this belongs a dying to sin and to the world, and to all inordinate delight of nature.'[1] But, as I have already pointed out, he is too well aware of the perils to the soul to encourage men to wish for or to speak of a death in love in the mystical rapture. Where he does write of the spirit being consumed and conquered and perishing in love (II xxi 2), he follows this immediately with the words 'our spirit and this love are living and fruitful in virtues'; and later he insists that if in Divine love we die to ourselves in God, we live in the spirit and savour the things that are eternal (II xxxiii). If we die to ourselves, we die to that in us which is alien to His nature; and if we live in Him, we live in our threefold unity of humanity, spirit and personality. Any other interpretation of his own words, or those of St. Paul, concerning 'dying' and 'uniting' lead directly to Pantheism: and he shows us in *The Little Book* how clearly he recognizes this. 'Behold, I have said thus, that the contemplative lover of God is united with God through means, and also without means, and thirdly without differentiation or perception of difference. And this I find in nature and in grace and also in glory. Behold, thus you must observe that we are united with God through means, both here in grace and also in glory. And in this mean there is great difference, both of life and of reward....
And St. Paul undoubtedly understood this when he said that he desired to be released from his body and to be with Christ.[2] But he did not say that he wished to be Christ Himself, nor

---

[1] *The Little Book, Werken* III 277.
[2] Philemon i 23.

God, as now some faithless and perverted men do, who say that they have no God, for they have died to themselves, and are united with God so that they have become God.'[1]

In *The Twelve Beguines* there is a similar affirmation, couched in the form of one of his favourite paradoxes: 'For the Spirit of God demands of our spirit that we at once surrender ourselves out of ourselves into God, and that we at once receive God into ourselves and comprehend Him: and both these things are impossible to us. For we cannot issue out of ourselves into God and lose our created nature; and so we must remain everlastingly different from God, and remain created creatures. For no creature can become God, nor can God become any creature.'[2] One cannot read such a passage without being struck by the lack which such doctrines as Pantheism display not so much of wisdom or knowledge as of common sense.

That such Pantheistic distortions of the truth lead directly to Quietism receives like recognition and denunciation. In *The Little Book* occurs the following passage: 'For in that highest realm to which they (Pantheists) have made their way, they feel nothing but their single being depending upon God's being. And they consider this single simplicity which they attain to be God, because in it they find natural rest. And therefore it seems to them that in the depths of their singleness they themselves are God. For they lack true faith, hope and love. And by means of the bare idleness which they feel and possess, so they say, they are without cognition and love and free of virtues. And therefore they are at pains to live without conscience, whatever evil they may do. And they are disobedient to all the sacraments and all virtues and all the exercises of Holy Church. For it seems to them that they have no need of this. But they say that imperfect men have need of this.'[3]

There can be no doubt either of the direction in which this is aimed, or of the relation between this false doctrine and

---

[1] *Werken* III 276–8.   [2] *Werken* IV 31.
[3] *Werken* III 279.

Ruysbroek's own teaching. In the first place, he patently has in mind the heretical Brethren of the Free Spirit, with their cultivation of complete passivity, their discouragement of all conscious practice of virtue, and their claim that 'no action can be sinful in the perfect', and also Eckhardt's proposition that 'the abandonment of our will to the permissive will of God excludes regret for our past sins'.[1]

We should compare this passage from *The Little Book* with Book II cap. xlii of the *Espousals*. Although the date of the *Espousals* is difficult to determine from internal evidence, recent scholarship has made a good case, in my opinion, for the thesis that it was begun at the time of Ruysbroek's retirement from Brussels, which followed immediately upon the termination of his campaign against Bloemardinne in 1343, and that it was completed only after his profession at Groenendael in 1351.[2] But even if the older view that when he began to write the *Espousals* he was already professed is correct, we can still see in this passage the plainest reflection of his experiences of the 'free spirit'. It would be possible to relate each point of his denunciation to, for example, the condemnation of the heretical tendencies among the Begards by the council of Vienna in 1311; but here it will suffice to deal with one point, Ruysbroek's demolition of 'false natural rest'.

Observe how, in the passage just quoted from *The Little Book*, he adds to his exposition of the Pantheists' belief that they themselves have become God, as it were by way of explanation, 'for they lack true faith, hope and love'. To him this is an adequate explanation of their fantastic dogma, and in the explanation is also the connecting link between Pantheism and Quietism. If such men, this sentence implies, had maintained justness and due proportion, and if they had sought a true unity with God, a unity of their personality and soul and humanity with Christ's, it would be impossible for them to believe that a mere passivity of their animal and spiritual natures, which should be active and yearning, could bring

[1] *Enthusiasm* pp. 239–40.
[2] *Werken* I xxxvii–xxxix; *Leven* 89.

them to unity with the Divine Personality; and faith and reason, which they do not exercise or seek, would teach them how absurd are their beliefs.

This 'false natural rest' of the Quietists he everywhere contrasts with the true rest of the soul, which is had in unity with God. There is no need to document or expound this matter farther; but it is appropriate that we should briefly examine some of the attributes of this rest, and notably its delectation, its lack of manner, its darkness and its not-knowing.

'Delectation' is the word I have used throughout to translate Ruysbroek's 'ghebruiken', which he employs in the same sense as the Latin 'fruitio'. I have preferred 'delectation' to 'fruition', because this second word today is so generally misunderstood and misused. Either term is inadequate, as inadequate as 'ghebruiken' itself, to convey what the author wants us to understand: and what this is he tries to define for us in *The Twelve Beguines*: 'All we who are one with God in love have delectation of Him, which is an empty, glorious, essential unity, without perception of difference of the Persons; there is neither the flowing-out nor the drawing-in of God; but there the Persons are empty and one in delectable love, which is an empty, glorious unity of the Persons. There rest, delectation and joy are illimitable. There all loving spirits are one blessed delectation without perception of difference. The delectation of God is unity of the Persons, naked emptiness, overflowing joy, unfathomable blessedness, the crown and reward in eternity of perfected love.'[1]

And from the *Espousals* we may glean several other indications of what Ruysbroek's meaning is. Thus, he tells us that whereas grace is given us for the sake of works, God gives us Himself, above rest, for the sake of delectation and rest (II vi). Similarly, we are told that delectation is without means (II xxi 1)—grace, it will be remembered, is itself a mean—and above time (I v): and we are also told that during His life upon earth, Christ's soul was preserved in rest and delectation by charity (I x).

[1] *Werken* IV 33.

From these indications and from the definition in *The Twelve Beguines*, it is possible to understand something of what Ruysbroek means, though he himself tells us, again and again, that to understand all that he means is impossible, for rest and delectation are beyond and above understanding and meaning. Delectation is not to be enjoyed by animal, sensual man: it is above time, in which humanity acts and feels, and without means, which work upon humanity and spirituality. And because delectation is without means and empty, naked, unfathomable, it is not to be enjoyed by spiritual man in his reason and intellect. But spiritual man's capacity for love is exalted by his personality to share the charity of God: and through charity he has in his personality rest and delectation, as in his spirituality he has love and intellectual cognition, and in his humanity the exercise of virtues, none of which can be perfect without the others.

In translating, I have throughout used 'charity' to render 'karitate', 'love' for 'minne'. From my translation it will be seen that Ruysbroek is not consistent in his use of these two words. He does not for example, use 'minne' to describe exclusively man's love for mankind, or for mankind and God: and there is certainly no equation of 'minne' with Eros, 'karitate' with Agape; but it is true to say that in speaking of God's love, he most often uses 'karitate', and that when he writes of man's 'karitate' he always means a godly love that reflects God's love. Indeed, I think that it is true to say that, for reasons which we have already examined, he is anxious in both terminology and argument to suggest as few analogies as possible between sacred and earthly love.

He tells us that, where God and the soul unite, charity is born (I v), and that Christ's charity flowed from the boundless well of the Holy Ghost (I x). Later, when he writes of the distinction to be drawn and observed between true and false intellectual attainment, he does not say that in orthodox Christianity the one is to be found, in heresy the other: instead, he tells us that we should judge clever men not by their cleverness but by their charity (II xvii 3). A single reading

3

of this last section is all that is needed to show us how deeply he was influenced by I Corinthians xiii: and again in II xli, where he is probably referring specifically to the excesses of the Begards, the argument is St. Paul's argument that it is useless for men to seek to immolate themselves if this is done for the sake of Eros and not of Agape.

This charity is not a mean, but an attribute of God Himself which we may share; and thus it is without means, and also 'without manner'. So I have translated Ruysbroek's 'onwise, wiseloes'. (Although I have deliberately refrained, in preparing this work, from consulting any English commentary or previous translation, I recall a suggestion of the late Evelyn Underhill, which I must have read some twenty years ago, that my 'with manner' should be rendered as 'somehow', and 'without manner' as 'nohow'. This is quite true, and I am well aware how often my translation has failed to convey Ruysbroek's felicity in finding simple, colloquial terms to convey abstract ideas to simple men and women: but if I had admitted 'somehow' and 'nohow' I should also have been obliged to admit 'whatness' for 'quiddity' and many other such locutions which would have annoyed and antagonized any reader of taste. When Ruysbroek is quaint, it is not for the sake of quaintness but of clarity, and I have sought to convey his clarity first, and his manner only second.)

He regards 'manner' as both an aid and a hindrance to progress in contemplation, which we must learn to use and to do without, just as we have seen in the case of images. Each virtue of Christ has its own special manner (I viii); that is, even Christ Himself is not 'without manner' in His virtuous, loving, suffering humanity. As Christ shared our humanity, so He practised virtue and exercised devotion, and in His soul He used His reason and intellect; and this practice, exercise and use are all of them 'manners', recognizable ways of progress for man. Manner is appropriate to the active life, Ruysbroek tells us; when man has attained to the perfection of the active life, he will reach a comprehension of Christ's active life and nature, of His manner and His works, and he will then seek to know what is His interior nature, His Spirit and Personality. It is this transference of our contemplation from manner to essence which marks the transition from the active life to the life of yearning (I xxxvi). This transition, and our abandonment of manner, in the life of yearning, as we cease to contemplate Christ's manner, he writes of again in *The Twelve Beguines*: 'And his love is so awful and so piercing and it so consumes all that it touches, (that) when we feel this, which is above reason, then our love is without manner and without fashion. For we cannot know how to respond to His love, which is so ravenous that it swallows and consumes in its own quality everything which comes near to it. Our love must give way to this love, for we cannot defend ourselves. For there indeed our love becomes naked, idle and without occupation. And the love of God is a consuming fire that ravishes us out of ourselves and swallows us up with God in unity.'[1]

It is not necessary to offer any explanation of Ruysbroek's images of 'nakedness', 'emptiness', 'bareness', which convey the meaning that in its union with God, human personality has passed beyond the exercise of the functions of humanity, and beyond all rational intellectual processes. This imagery, and its ancestry, will be familiar to all who know his great contemporary, the author of *The Cloud of Unknowing*. But concerning one other related image, that of 'darkness', it may be well to write briefly, because its use by Ruysbroek, and, following him, by St. John of the Cross, is so often misunderstood, misinterpreted and misquoted. Ruysbroek and St. John do not at all intend us to understand by this image any conception of doubt, despair, or tribulation: such afflictions are a well-recognized feature of the way of contemplation, and Ruysbroek deals with them in their proper place; but in writing of them, he compares the time in which man is so afflicted to a desert, parched and waterless, itself a figure of respectable ancestry. When he first comes to speak of darkness (in II xxxvi), we are already well prepared for the value to be given to this symbol by his previous use of such paradoxical figures as the

[1] *Werken* IV 33.

woe and torment that are the greatest of all joys, the hunger and thirst that feast daily on every delicacy and are yet never appeased. They are informed by his vision and knowledge of the greatest paradox of all, the vision of God which is more perceptible and comprehensible than anything to which feeling and reason can attain, and which is yet in its essence imperceptible and incomprehensible. On the other hand, Christ is likened again and again to the sun, His working on our spiritual and physical powers to the sun's vivifying influence upon the earth. When finally in Book III Ruysbroek writes of the darkness for what it truly is, it is to tell us that in darkness, that is, beyond feeling and reason, we receive an incomprehensible light which is Christ.

We must refer this concept of darkness and not-knowing, and Ruysbroek's consequent views upon the finite nature of human wisdom and reason, to his doctrine of the essential nature and function of human existence. We are humanity, spirit and personality: God has endowed our humanity with senses, with which we are to feel, and our spirituality with reason, with which we are to think: and it is our nature and duty to pursue the active life of feeling and devotion, and the yearning life of reasoning and perception. In our attainment of the third life, the life of contemplation, feeling and reasoning are united and exalted to union with God, above devotion and above perception. Devotion and the senses, reasoning and the intellect cannot and should not be abandoned; but just as it is not possible for us to 'think with our blood' (the phrase of a twentieth-century novelist whom the twentieth century thinks fit to style a mystic) or to feel with our intellect, so it is not possible to have union with God and to know Him through sense and thought, which are incapable of comprehending Him.

This doctrine was put for Ruysbroek and is put for us, with a concision which Ruysbroek rarely attempts, by St. Paul: 'Things no eye has seen, no ear has heard, no human heart conceived, the welcome God has prepared for those who love Him. To us, then, God has made a revelation of it through

His Spirit; there is no depth in God's nature so deep that the Spirit cannot find it out. Who else can know a man's thoughts, except the man's own spirit that is within him? So no one else can know God's thoughts, but the Spirit of God. Mere man with his natural gifts cannot take in the thoughts of God's Spirit . . . whereas the man who has spiritual gifts can scrutinize everything, without being subject, himself, to any other man's scrutiny.'[1]

This underlies all that Ruysbroek has to say of human wisdom and reason. One must not seek to understand God's mysteries: they are to be accepted through faith, not through comprehension (I xxviii). We should observe carefully the context of this, the discussion of sobriety: I have already pointed out the relevance of this treatment in Book I of the theological virtues to Ruysbroek's views on the nature and origins of heresy. If Bloemardinne and the Begards had preserved sobriety, had they not sought 'to taste and know the things that are not permitted' (I xxviii)—that is, not permitted to the senses and reason—they would not have confused the false rest of nature and the senses with the true rest in God which is above nature.

He makes a similar point in dealing with purity (I xxix). The pure man will cleave only to God, and not to any of His creatures: and so his cleaving will be beyond the understanding and beyond the senses. This, too, has a direct application to Quietism, 'seraphic love' and like perversions: no acknowledgment that we as humans are finite is to lead us to regard ourselves as not bound by the laws of perfection.

The highest recognition of God to which man can attain in the active life, and that by faith, is the mystery of comprehending Him to be incomprehensible (I xxxvi). Similarly, as man proceeds by way of the life of yearning to the life of contemplation, the reason, illumined, exalts the spirit in inward perception, but the ensuing vision of the Godhead will blind and silence reason and observation (II xxi). It is man's capacity for loving which will press on; his reason is locked out (II xxi 1);

[1] I Corinthians ii 9–16.

and already in Book I we have been told that to recognize God and to see Him without love has neither savour nor profit to man (I xxxiii).

None the less, Ruysbroek is careful to point out that there is nothing in this doctrine of not-knowing which imputes blame to those who do not advance beyond the active or the yearning life: few men can do so, and those who cannot should neither trouble themselves on this account, nor disparage those who do (III, prologue). What, then, must the many do who are not chosen? They must do their best in the active life, and in the yearning life if grace is vouchsafed them, and in all things they must keep to the high road, by which, he is at pains to remind us, we can only at all times understand submission to the authority of the Church. Our Redeemer Himself was obedient to the laws and even to the conventions, the 'sacramentals' of Judaism (I ix); and so ought we to be to His laws and His Church, observing how daily He comes to us in the sacraments which the Church ensures to us (I xiv), and in perfect, Christlike humility showing reverence to Church and sacraments (I xix).

Ruysbroek himself would have said that in thus providing that his teachings were applicable and comfortable to all men, he was being 'common': this term is the 'indifferent' of the Book of Common Prayer, the impartiality which is an attribute of Divine charity, as is indivisibility of Trinity. God is 'a common light' (I iii), and in all His attributes He is 'common and outflowing' (II xvi). 'God is common with all His gifts. The angels are common. The soul is common in all its powers and in all the body and in all the limbs . . .' (II xvi): and again we should observe the passage beginning 'Now mark how Christ gave Himself in common . . .' (II xvii 4). When man goes out from the unity of the spirit, he is in his unity and in his going-out to reflect the Divine nature, and to be common, and to go out to God and His saints, to sinners and those in error, to the holy souls in purgatory and to himself and all good men on earth (II xvii 2).

This is the 'common life' of impartial love, of adoration and intercession and expostulation, which gave name and form to

the devotees who grouped themselves around Ruysbroek's
disciple Geert Groote[1]: the Brethren of the Common Life took
the *Espousals* as their rule, and we can find the origins of their
zeal for reform as well as of their devotions, the 'devotio
moderna', in Ruysbroek. They denounced the infamy of the
lives of clerics and bishops, as he does, for example, in the
bitter words with which he compares the 'common' church
to which Christ bequeathed His treasure, to be held in common
for all, with the churchmen of his day, avaricious, unenlightened, luxurious. And as Ruysbroek was, so were the Brethren
of the Common Life accused of heresy: there must indeed have
been much in Groote's sensational preaching campaigns and
the multitudinous conversions he effected to remind ordinaries
of Bloemardinne and others who had disturbed not only their
own rest and quiet but the peace and unity of the Church; but
the Brethren's reputation in the end survived such charges,
as Ruybroek's did.

In his teaching and in his whole intellectual development,
Ruysbroek himself perfectly exemplifies his own doctrine of
'commonness'. Pauline, Augustinian, Thomist, he is able as
is the bee of his simile to gather sweetness from every flower
and bring it to the use and profit of the commonwealth: no-one,
reading only his adroit handling of the doctrines of free-will
(to which he is much devoted) and predestination (which he
prefers not to elaborate), could guess how in his own day and to
his own knowledge Christendom was still shaken and convulsed
by the thunders and lightnings of this debate. Nor does he
leave us room to dub him 'theocentric' or 'Christocentric':
rapt as he is in his contemplation of a Godhead in which the
Persons of the Trinity Themselves have no 'discretion', he
matches in his devotion to the Redeemer that of the most
fervent 'Christocentric' mystics of his age, anticipating, as he
so often seems to do, the devotions to the Sacred Heart and to
the Body of Christ which we associate first with the century
after his death. He is not 'liturgical' (at least, not in the
Espousals), but even here, when he paraphrases the prayer of

[1] See *Leven*, pp. 134–40.

37

consecration from the Canon of the Mass (II xvii 4), he shows us how the liturgy was a part of his life and thought.

He tries to tell us nothing of what he was, yet the *Espousals* alone gives us a picture of the man more living than any formal confession could be. Full of natural curiosity, he can tell us how trees are grafted, of the habits of the bee, the ant and the bat, of the 'houses' of the firmament and the motion of the planets, what is the progress of fevers, what are the symptoms of dropsy, what is the effect of honey-dew upon the crops, what is the action of boiling water: and we can imagine the studious, careful, profitable days of observation and speculation which he passed at Groenendael, in the orchard and the kitchen and the infirmary, as well as in the library.

In his approach to philosophy he is perfectly a man of his own times. From the schools and his own studies he has brought away a deep love of logic, not for its own sake but for its power to refine and sift and select, to bring method and discipline to the work of discerning true from false among the conclusions of human intellect. He clearly recognizes the importance of instinct, sense and emotion in the progress towards illumination, but he does not expect them to do the work of the intellect, nor the finite human intellect to be capable of comprehending a Divine infinity. If we find somewhat tedious the reiteration of the various syllogisms which are the steps that his argument mounts, we must remember that he as a good teacher wished at all times to keep his pupils informed not only of his conclusions but also of the method by which he arrived at them, and also that, for his more advanced readers, the method itself had an allurement which he knew and would hardly wish to forgo. Numbers, categories and order had for medieval man an emotional as well as an intellectual significance: in part this may reflect his need to harmonize the apparent chaos of the observable world with his conviction that creation corresponds with the essentially harmonious nature of its Creator. The whole of the *Espousals* is constructed upon such principles of order, balance and symmetry. There are, indeed, many resemblances between Ruysbroek's art and that of the musician of his day. In his thought and in his language he takes delight in constructing a figure, and then, with mathematical care and ingenuity, devising variations which are, to one another and to their original figure, as harmonious as the voices in a canon. Nowhere is this better illustrated than in the harmony of structure to be observed between Books I, II and III: the candid simplicity of the first, the majestic and complex progress of the second and the terseness, elusive and evocative, of the third are all built upon the same logical structure, so that we may say of the three books, as their author says of the consummations of the three lives of which they treat, that no one may perfectly be comprehended without the others.

The *Espousals* demands of its readers the same exercise of all their faculties and gifts of which it so often treats. Its appeal is at once intellectual and emotional, nor is it easy to distinguish one from the other. The response of the reader to repetition and variation, rhythm and balance, both in argument and in language, was intended to be in part a response of the reason to a series of philosophic demonstrations, in part a response of the emotions to a devotional work of art.

This art, furthermore, is Ruysbroek's own. Great though his debt was to St. Paul, St. Augustine, St. Thomas Aquinas, the Victorines of Paris and others, and even though the use of the vernacular as a means of instruction was already traditional in the Low Countries, still Ruysbroek gained for himself his 'miraculous' reputation for the ease and felicity with which his thought seems to grow and clothe itself in his own words. His books are a world removed from the tricks that bedizen the popular tract and sermon of his time: we shall look in vain in them for the *exemplum*; and it is only rarely, as in the figures of the branches of the tree of Faith or of the parti-coloured robe of Free Will, that we know that here we have a rhetorical device which the centuries have robbed of its potency.

In his language, Ruysbroek is rare even among the mystics, who so often warn us how inadequate and misleading are the symbols they are forced to employ. Sometimes we have a hint of Ruysbroek's fears concerning this, but they seem rather to be fears for the inadequacy of his readers, who may prove to be crude and insensitive (II xi 2), or who may allow themselves to be beguiled by merely corporeal images, too easily expressed in words (II xi 3). But his language as such he appears to find adequate, so far as any sensual and intellectual means may be, to convey his thoughts to his own satisfaction; and at its best, as in his figure of the contention in the storm of love of the two spirits (II xxi 2), we have the work of a poet, a poet of an order far higher than is revealed by his pleasing, homely, unambitious verses in *The Twelve Beguines*, for example, work which cannot be reinterpreted or paraphrased or translated without damaging the original.

But Ruysbroek himself would undoubtedly have rejected such claims to intellectual and artistic pre-eminence, not through any false modesty, but because he esteemed such things little when weighed against virtue and devotion, charity and truth. The conclusion of *The Little Book* tells better than I can do how he wished to be remembered: 'In all things which I understand or feel or have written, I submit myself to the judgment of the saints and of Holy Church: for I will live and die as the servant of Jesus Christ, in the Christian Faith. And I long to be by the grace of God a living branch of Holy Church. And therefore, as I have said to you before, you should hold yourselves aloof from those men who are in their empty ignorance so deceived that crassly and foolishly they believe that out of their own natures they have found within themselves the indwelling of God, and who wish to be one with God without His grace and without the exercise of virtue, and in disobedience to God and to Holy Church. And they wish by nature to be the sons of God, as do all those of whom I have spoken who live in error. And since the prince of angels was cast out of heaven because he vaunted himself and wished to be equal to God, and the first man was driven out of Paradise because he wished to be like to God, how then shall the most evil sinner, which is the faithless Christian, come to heaven from earth, who wishes to be God Himself, but not to equal Him in grace and virtue?

For no-one can by his own strength climb up to heaven, save only the Son of Man, Jesus Christ. And therefore we must unite ourselves with Him through grace and virtue and Christian belief, and so with Him we shall climb to where He has gone before. For on the last day we shall all arise, each one in his own body. And then those who have done good works shall go into eternal life, and those who have done evil works shall go into eternal fire. These are two regions unlike each other, and nevermore to be united; for each is ever averse from the other. Pray and desire for him who has composed and written this, that God be merciful to him: that he and all of us be brought, out of our wretched beginnings and our miserable continuation, to a blessed end. May Jesus Christ, the living Son of God, grant that to us all. Amen.'[1]

[1] *Werken* III 297–8.

THE PROLOGUE

Concerning a spiritual espousal between God and our humanity

'SEE, the Bridegroom comes: go out to meet Him.'[1] St. Matthew the Evangelist writes these words for us, and Christ spoke them to His disciples and to all men, as we may read in the parable of the virgins. This Bridegroom is Christ, and man's nature is the bride, whom God has made in the image and the likeness of Himself. And in the beginning He had set her in the highest place, and in the fairest and richest and most splendid of dwellings, that was in paradise. And to her He had subjected all creatures, and He had adorned her with graces, and to her He had given a commandment: and had she showed obedience, she would have deserved to live steadfast and secure in everlasting wedlock with her Bridegroom and never to fall into any distress or sin.

Then there came a knave, the fiend from hell, cunningly in the guise of a serpent, and he was envious of this and he deceived the woman, and the two of them deceived the man, in whom humanity first existed. And by false counsel he seduced her, Nature, the bride of God. And she was driven out into a strange land, poor and wretched, and was made prisoner and oppressed and enslaved by her foes, as if she should never return to her native land or have pardon.

But when God thought it time, and when He had pity on this anguish of His subjects, then He sent His only-begotten Son on earth, into a splendid court and into a glorious temple, which was the body of the glorious maiden Mary. There He espoused this bride, our nature, and united her with His Person by the noble virgin's most pure blood. The priest who

[1] St. Matthew xxv 6.

blessed the bride, that was the Holy Ghost. The angel Gabriel brought the command. The glorious maiden gave the consent.

Thus has Christ, our plighted Bridegroom, united our nature with Him, and has visited us in a strange land, and has taught us with heavenly laws and with the uttermost faith. And He has laboured and striven as a champion against our foes, and He has broken open the prison and has won the battle, and by His death has dealt death to our death, and has ransomed us with His blood and has set us free with the waters of His baptism, and has enriched us with His sacraments and His gifts, so that we may go out clad in all virtues, as He says, and meet Him in the court of glories, and enjoy Him without end and evermore.

Now Christ, the master teaching truth, says: 'See, the Bridegroom comes, go out to meet Him.' In these words Christ our true love teaches us four things. First, He gives us a command, in that He says 'See'. Those who shut their eyes and neglect this command, they are all condemned. In the next words He shows us what we shall see, that is the coming of the Bridegroom. Then thirdly He teaches us and commands what we should do, in that He says 'Go out'. Fourthly, when He says 'To meet Him', He makes plain to us the profit and use of all our labour and all our life, that is, a loving meeting with the Bridegroom.

Let us expound and make plain these words in three manners. First, according to common usage, as they concern the life of the beginner, which is called active life, needful to all men who wish to be saved. Next let us make plain the same words as they concern the interior, exalted, yearning life which many men achieve by virtues and the grace of God. Thirdly, let us illumine them as they concern the supernatural life of the contemplation of God, which a few men can achieve in this manner or can savour, by way of their exalted and excellent form of living.

BOOK ONE

THE ACTIVE LIFE

PART ONE

'See': the three conditions necessary for seeing

Now for the first matter. Christ, the wisdom of the Father, speaks and has spoken, inwardly according to His Divinity, and has said to all men since Adam's days: 'See'. And we have need of seeing. Now mark well: so that we may see with bodily or with spiritual eye, three things are necessary.

A. IN ORDER TO SEE WITH THE BODILY EYE (*cap. i*)

Firstly, if men shall see with bodily eye that which is around them, then they must have from without the light of heaven, or some other material light, so that the medium, which is the air, may be illumined there where they are to see. The second necessity is that of their own free will they allow the things which they are to see to form images in their eyes. The third is that the instruments, the eyes, be sound and without flaw, so that rude and material objects may in them keenly be reflected. Should one of these three be lacking in a man, then his bodily sight will be defective. But let us say no more of this seeing, but speak of a spiritual, supernatural seeing, in which reposes all our blessedness.

B. IN ORDER TO SEE WITH THE SPIRITUAL EYE (*cap. ii*)

Whoever shall see supernaturally has need of three conditions, which are: the light of the grace of God, and a will that is freely turned to Him, and a conscience not afflicted with deadly sin.

4   47

a. *God's offer of grace to all men (cap. iii)*

So now observe: since God is a common good, and since His unfathomable love is common, He therefore imparts His grace in two manners: preventive grace, and the grace by which men gain eternal life.

All men have His preventive grace in common, heathen and Jews, good and bad. Through the common love which God has to all men, He has caused His name and His redemption to be proclaimed and revealed to human beings in every quarter of the earth. He may convert every man who wishes to turn. All the sacraments, that of baptism and the other sacraments, are at hand to all men who wish to receive them, each according to his need. For God wishes to preserve all men, and to lose no single one. For on the Day of Judgment no man shall be able to complain against Him that not enough was done for him, for he could have wished to turn. For God is a common light, illumining heaven and earth and each man according to his need and his worth.

But though God is common, and though the sun shines equally upon all trees, many a tree still remains barren, and yet another tree bears rich fruit, to the great profit of men. That is why men are accustomed to cut trees open and to graft them with slips cut from fertile trees, so that they too bear good fruit, of a good flavour and profitable to men. The light of the grace of God is a fruitful branch, coming from the living paradise of the everlasting kingdom. There is no deed which may be of good flavour or of profit to men which does not grow from this branch: and this branch of the grace of God, which makes men pleasing to God, since by it men deserve eternal life, it is offered to all men, but yet it is not planted in all men. This is because they will not prune their tree of its wild growth, that is, their unbelief, or their perverted disobedience against the commandments of God.

But if this branch of the grace of God is to be planted in our soul, to this end three things are necessary: the preventive grace of God, and a will that is freely turned to Him, and a

48

clean conscience. Preventive grace reaches all men, for it is God Who gives it. But a willing conversion and the cleansing of the conscience are not given to all men, and therefore they lack the grace of God, in which they should deserve eternal life.

b. *How God works in all men by means of preventive grace* (*cap. iv*)

Preventive grace reaches man from without or from within. From without through sicknesses, or through the loss of temporal possessions, of kinsmen or of friends: or because of public disgrace; or else a man is touched by sermons, or by the good examples of saints or good men, their words, it may be, or their deeds, so that he recognizes himself for what he is. So God reaches man from without. Sometimes too man is touched from within, in meditating upon the Passion and the merits of Our Lord, and on the benefits which God has conferred upon him and all men; or in contemplating his sins, the shortness of this life, and the terrors of death and hell: the everlasting torments of hell and the everlasting joys of heaven: and that God has spared him while he lived in sin, and has waited for his conversion: or he observes the marvel which God has created in all creatures on earth or in heaven. These are the works of preventive grace, which move men from without or from within in many ways.

And man has also a natural inclination towards good by means of the sudden illumining of the soul and the *ratio superior*, so that always he desires the good and hates the bad. In these ways God touches all men according to their wants, and each man according to his needs, so that by these means man is struck sometimes and accused in his conscience and terrified and put in torment, and remains shut up in himself, regarding nothing but himself. This is not antecedent grace, nor is it meritorious: but in this way preventive grace makes us ready to receive those other graces by means of which men deserve eternal life. When the soul thus remains free of evil will and evil deeds, and conscious of its iniquity and struck down and in torment over what it ought to do, mindful of God and of itself and of its evil deeds, there proceeds from this a natural loathing for sin, and a natural good will. This is the highest of the preventive graces.

c. *The co-operation of God and man in justification* (*cap. v*)

When man has done all that he is able, and can do no more because of his own feebleness, then there is need of the immeasurable riches of God, that they may finish the work. So there comes from above the light of the grace of God, just as a ray from the sun, and it is sent suddenly into the soul, but not through any merit or desire. For in this light God gives to man His free riches and liberality, God Whom no creature may deserve before he possesses Him. And this is God's secret working in the soul, above time, and it moves the soul and all its powers. This is the end of preventive grace, and the beginning of the second, that is the supernatural light. The light is the first point, and from it springs the second point, which is for the soul to do: that is, a free turning of the will, in a moment of time; and from this there springs charity in the uniting of God and the soul. These two points hang together, so that the one cannot be completed without the other. Where God and the soul meet together in the unity of love, there God gives the light of His grace above time; and the soul gives its free conversion, by means of the power of grace, in a brief instant of time; and there charity is born in the soul, of God and of the soul; for charity is the lovers' bond between God and the loving soul.

Out of these two points, that is out of the grace of God and out of a free turning of the will illumined with grace, there springs charity, that is Divine love; and out of Divine love there springs the third point, which is a cleansing of the conscience. These points so converge that one of them may not persist without the other for any time, for whoever has Divine love has perfect contrition for sin. Yet here men may perceive the ordinance of God and also of His creatures, for God gives His light, and in this light man gives a willing and complete conversion: out of these two proceeds a perfect love towards God, and out of love proceeds perfect contrition and cleansing of the conscience, and that takes place as man looks down upon the wrong-doing and the defilement of the soul. Because man loves well, there comes in him a dislike of himself and all his works. So it is ordained in the converted. From this there comes an anxious contrition and a perfect sorrow that he ever did transgress, and a fervent desire never again to sin and evermore to serve God in devoted obedience; careful confession, free from concealment and ambiguity and dissembling; perfect penance following the advice of a skilled priest; and then to begin a life of virtue and all good works.

These three points, then, as you have heard, belong necessarily to a godly life. If you have these three points, then Christ speaks in you: See, and may it be that you truly see.

This is the first point in the four principles which Christ our Lord enunciates: See.

PART TWO

'The Bridegroom Comes'. Of the threefold coming of Christ which is to be looked for (cap. vi)

Now He makes plain what we shall see, when He says: 'The Bridegroom comes'. In the Latin, Christ our Bridegroom uses this word *venit*. This word unites in itself two different times: the time that is past, and the time that is now present: and yet furthermore He refers to the time which is to come. And in this regard we should notice the three comings of our Bridegroom Jesus Christ. He came first when He became man for the sake of mankind, out of love. The second coming takes place every day, again and again, in every loving heart, with new graces, with new gifts, according to men's capacity for receiving. In the third we see His coming to judgment, or at the hour of death. In all these comings of Our Lord, and in all His works, three things are to be noticed: the cause and wherefore, the manner from within, and the work from without.

A. THE FIRST COMING, WHEN GOD BECOMES MAN

a. *The reason of this coming (cap. vii)*

The wherefore, the reason why God created the angels and men, was His unfathomable goodness and greatness, for He wished so to do that the blessedness and the riches which are Himself might be revealed to rational beings, so that they might taste of Him within time, and delight in Him above time in eternity. The reason why God became man, that was His incomprehensible love and the need of all men: for they were ruined by our forefather's fall, and they could not set it to rights. But the reason why Christ according to His Divinity and also according to His humanity performed all His works on earth, this reason is fourfold, that is: His Divine love which is immeasurable; and the created love which is called charity, which He had in His soul together with the uniting of the everlasting word and the perfect gifts of His Father; and the great need of human nature; and the honour of His Father. These are the reasons for the coming of Christ our Bridegroom, and of all His works, inward and outward.

b. *The manner and the operation of this coming (cap. viii)*

Now it behoves us to observe in Christ our Bridegroom, so that we may wish to follow Him in virtues according to our power, the manner of His interior life, and the exterior works which He performed: that is to say, His virtue and His works of virtue. The manner of His life was according to His Divinity, and this manner is to us unattainable and incomprehensible. For that is because He is eternally born of the Father and because the Father in Him and through Him acknowledges and creates and orders and rules all things in heaven and in earth. For He is the wisdom of the Father. And they breathe one Spirit, a love which is a bond uniting the two of them, and all saints and all good men in heaven and on earth. Let us speak no more of this manner, but of that manner which Christ used by Divine gifts and according to His created humanity. There is indeed much to be said of this manner, for Christ had as many interior manners as He had interior virtues: because each virtue has its own special manner. These virtues and these manners were in Christ's soul so that it is above the understanding and the comprehension of all creatures. But let us consider three, that is: humility and charity, and passion or suffering, inward and outward, in patience. These are the three chief roots and beginnings of all virtue and all perfection.

1. *The first manner: Christ's humility, according to His Divinity and humanity (cap. ix)*

Now understand: in Christ, by reason of His Divinity, men find two kinds of humility. The first is that He was willing to become man, and that He was willing to take upon Him human nature, that nature that was rejected and accursed into the very depths of hell, and that He was willing in His entire person to be one with it, so that every man, bad or good, may say: Christ, the Son of God, is my brother. The second humility, according to His Divinity, is that He chose a poor virgin, not a king's daughter, to be His mother, and so that the poor virgin should be the mother of God, ruler of heaven and earth and all creatures. Furthermore, one may say of all the acts of humility which Christ ever performed, that God performed them.

But now let us consider the humility that was in Christ according to His humanity, and by means of graces and Divine gifts. Thus His soul with all its might was bowed down in reverence and in worship before the great power of the Father: for a heart bowed down is a humble heart. Therefore He performed all His works to the honour and praise of His Father, nor did He in any thing seek to glorify His humanity. He was humble and obedient to the older dispensation and to the commandments, and at times to conventions, when that was profitable. And for that reason He was circumcised and taken to the Temple and presented according to custom, and He paid taxes to the emperor as did other Jews. And He was humble and obedient to His mother and to St. Joseph. And therefore He served them, according to all their orders, with ready submission. He chose poor outcasts for His companions, to wander through the world converting it: these were the apostles, and among them and among all men He was lowly and humble. And thus for this reason He was at the bidding of all men, in whatever need they were, whether of heavenly things or earthly, just as if He were the lackey of the whole world. This is the first point concerning the humility of Christ our Bridegroom.

2. *The second manner : Christ's charity, adorned with all virtues (cap. x)*

Concerning the second point, which was charity, beginning and source of all virtues. This charity preserved the highest power of His soul in a stillness and in an enjoyment of that very blessedness which He now enjoys. And this same charity exalted Him evermore to His Father, with reverence, with love, with praise, with worship, with inward prayer for the needs of all men, with offering up of all His deeds to the honour of His Father.

Yet this same charity caused Christ to abase Himself to the material and spiritual needs of all men, faithful and kind as a lover; and here He gave by His life an example to all men of how they should live. He nourished all men: their spirits within, as they might receive it, with true teaching, and their senses from without with miracles and wonders. And sometimes too He fed them with food for the body, as when they followed Him into the wilderness and could go no farther. He made the deaf to hear and the blind to see, the dumb to speak and the fiend to flee out of men; He made the dead live and cripples to walk straight; and this one must interpret literally and spiritually. Christ our Lover has laboured for us, interiorly and exteriorly, in true and faithful manner: we may never comprehend the depths of His charity, for it flowed from the boundless well of the Holy Ghost, and in measure above that of all who ever experienced charity, for He was God and man in one person. This is the second point, concerning charity.

3. *The third manner: Christ's Passion and sufferings, in patience, to death (cap. xi)*

The third point concerns suffering in patience. We must earnestly observe this point, for it adorned Christ our Bridegroom in all His life. For at the very moment of His birth He began to suffer; and He suffered poverty and cold. He was circumcised and shed His blood; He was sent fleeing into a strange land; He served St. Joseph and His mother; He endured hunger and thirst, contempt and reviling, and the shameful words and deeds of the Jews; He fasted, He watched and He was tempted by the devil. He was made subject to all men. He wandered from region to region and from place to place, preaching the Gospel with great labour and great care. At last

He was taken captive by the Jews, they who were the enemies of Him who loved them. He was betrayed, mocked and ridiculed, scourged and buffeted, condemned through false witness. He carried His cross with great woe up to the highest place upon earth. He was stripped mother-naked. Never did man or woman see so fair a body so misused. He suffered shame, pain and cold before all the world: He was naked and it was cold, and the bitter wind blew into His wounds. He was nailed to the wood of the cross with rude nails, and racked so that His veins burst. He was dragged up and cast down so that His wounds bled. His head was crowned with thorns; His ears heard the cruel Jews cry 'Crucify Him, crucify Him', and many an unworthy word; His eyes beheld the Jews, set as one man upon their wickedness, and the desolation of His mother, and in the bitterness of His torment and death His sight failed; His nostrils breathed in the foulness of their spittle upon His face; His mouth and His throat were drenched with vinegar and gall: His whole being tormented through and through: Christ our Bridegroom brought by torment to death, forsaken by God and by all creatures, dying as He hung upon the cross, as it were an image heeded by no-one, except for Mary His mother, who could not help Him.

Yet more Christ suffered in His soul from the wilful obstinacy of all the Jews and of those who slew Him: for whatever signs and wonders they saw, they persisted in their wickedness. And He suffered for their damnation and for the vengeance because of His death; for God would inflict vengeance upon them, soul and body. And still He suffered on account of the lamentation and the desolation of His mother and His disciples, who were in great affliction. And He suffered because His death should be lost to so many men, and because of the ingratitude of many men, and because of the evil which would afflict many, to the reproach and shame of Him who died for love of us. And His humanity and His *ratio inferior* suffered, since God withdrew from them the benefits of His gifts and His comfort, and left them solitary in such need: and it was of this that Christ complained and said: 'My

God, my God, why hast Thou forsaken me?'.[1] Christ our
Lover kept silence over all His own sufferings, and cried out
to His Father: 'Father, forgive them, for they know not what
they do'.[2] Christ was heard by His Father because of His piety,[3]
since those who acted out of ignorance were thereafter soon
converted.

This was the manner of Christ's interior Passion, humility,
charity and suffering in patience. These three Christ our
Bridegroom maintained through all His life, and in His death;
and He paid our debt in His justice, and in His love He
opened His side. And from it there flowed the abounding
rivers, the sacraments of blessedness. And He ascended in
glory, and sits at the right hand of His Father, and reigns in
eternity.

This is the first coming of our Bridegroom, which has
perfectly come to pass.

B. THE SECOND, DAILY COMING, IN MAN'S SOUL (*cap. xii*)

The second coming of Christ our Bridegroom happens every
day in good men, ever and again, with graces and with new
gifts, in all those who dispose themselves to this according to
their powers. Here let us not speak of the first conversion of
men, nor of the first graces given to them when they turn
themselves from sin to virtue. But let us speak of their growth
in new graces and in new virtues from day to day, and of a
present coming of Christ our Bridegroom, daily in our soul.
Now it is for us to observe the cause and the reason, the manner
and the works of this coming.

a. *The reason, the manner and the operation of this coming, in an image of the sun in the valley (cap. xiii)*

There are four reasons: God's pity, and our necessity; God's
mildness, and our longings. These four cause virtue and

[1] St. Matthew xxvi 46.   [2] St. Luke xxiii 34.   [3] Cf. Hebrews v 7.

excellence to grow. Now understand: when the sun sends its rays and its light into a deep valley between two high mountains, and the sun then stands in the height of the firmament, so that it can illuminate the floor and the depths of the valleys, then three things take place. The valley is given more light, and light is reflected from the mountains, and there is more heat: and it becomes more fertile than flat and even land. And in just the same way, when a good man reflects in the depths of his being upon his littleness, and acknowledges that he has nothing and is nothing and can do nothing of his own power, he cannot remain still, nor can he advance in virtues; and when he acknowledges also that he frequently lacks virtues and good works, in this he acknowledges his poverty and his need, and so he makes a valley of humility. And because he is then humble and in need, and because he confesses his need, he thus shows and laments his need of the riches and pity of God. So he perceives how high God is, and how low he is; and so he is a deep valley. And Christ is a Sun of righteousness, and also of mercy, standing in the height of the firmament, that is at the right hand of His Father, and He shines into the depths of the humble heart: for Christ is altogether moved by men's need when they humbly call on Him and lament. Then there grow in that place two mountains, which is a twofold desire: the desire to serve and praise God in worship, and the second desire, to win virtues in excellence. These two mountains are higher than heaven, for these desires touch God immediately and call on His generous pity. Because then God's pity cannot restrain itself but must flow, for the soul then is able to have and to receive more gifts. This is the cause of the new coming of Christ, with new virtues for the soul. Then this valley, the humble heart, experiences three things: it is more illumined and enlightened with graces, and more warmed in charity, and made more fruitful in perfect virtues and in good works. And thus you have the reason and the manner and the works of this coming.

b. *The strengthening and making steadfast of the operation, through Christ's coming in the sacraments (cap. xiv)*

There is yet another coming of Christ our Bridegroom, which takes place each day in multiplication of graces and in new gifts, that is when man receives one of the sacraments, with humble heart and with a proper disposition, he so receives new gifts and greater grace through humility and through the heavenly secret working of Christ in the sacrament. Lack of a proper disposition is to say lack of faith in baptism, of penitence in confession, to approach the sacrament of the altar in mortal sin or with evil will, and so forth with the other sacraments. Such as do so receive no new grace, but rather sin the more. This is the second coming of Christ our Bridegroom, which now is present among us each day. And we should mark this with devout hearts till it come to pass in us. For there is need of it, if we are to persist or advance in the eternal life.

C. OF THE THIRD COMING OF OUR LORD TO JUDGMENT.

a. *The reason of this coming (cap. xv)*

The third coming, which is still to happen, is His coming to judgment, or in the hour of our death. The reasons for this coming shall be the fittingness of the time, the opportunity of the case and the judge's justice. The fitting time for this coming is at the hour of death and at the last judgment of all men. When God created the soul out of nothing, and united with the body, He set a determined day and a certain hour for it, and these are only known to Him, and then the soul must relinquish time, and reveal itself in His presence. The opportunity of the case is required because the soul must speak and answer for the words and all the works that ever it performed, in the presence of the eternal verity. The justice of the judge is required, because to Christ belong judgment and sentence, for He is the Son of Man and the Wisdom of the Father, to which

Wisdom all judgment belongs. For to Wisdom all hearts are plain and open, in heaven and earth and hell. And therefore these three points shall be the circumstances of the general advent on the last day, and also of the special advent to each man in the hour of his death.

b. *The manner and the operation of this coming (cap. xvi)*

The manner in which Christ our Bridegroom and our Judge shall act in this judgment is that He will reward and punish according to justice, for He gives to each man according to his deserts. He gives to good men for every good work which is done in God's name an unmeasured reward, that is Himself Whom no creature can deserve. But since He co-operates in His creatures in their good works, each creature earns Him as a reward, according to his powers, and that with a proportionate justice. To the damned He gives everlasting woe and torment, because they have despised and rejected an everlasting good for the sake of a good that is transitory. And of their own free will they have turned away from God, to His dishonour and against His will, and they have turned themselves to His creatures. And with justice they are condemned. Those who bear witness at the judgment are the angels and men's conscience. And the opposing advocate is the devil of hell, and the judge is Christ, Whom no man may deceive.

c. *Of five sorts of men who shall come to judgment (cap. xvii)*

There are five sorts of people who must appear before this judge. The first class, and the worst, are those Christian men who die in mortal sin without contrition and without repentance, because they have despised the death of Christ and His sacraments, or have received them vainly and without proper disposition. And they have not shown works of mercy in charity to their fellow-Christians according to God's ordinance, and therefore they are condemned to the nethermost pit in hell. The next class are those without the Faith, heathens or Jews. They must all appear before Christ. Yet they were condemned all the days of their lives, for they had neither grace nor Divine love: therefore they dwelt always in the everlasting death of damnation. But they shall be less tormented than evil Christians, because they had received fewer gifts from God and knew less of what they owed to God. The third class are good Christians who sometimes have fallen into sin, and have risen up again with contrition and acts of penance, and have not fulfilled their penance as justice required. Their place is in purgatory. The fourth class are those who have kept God's commandments, or, even if they have broken them, have turned again to God with contrition and with penitence and with works of charity and mercy, and have completed their penance, so that their souls, issuing forth, go straight to heaven without any purgation. The fifth class are those who have their conversation in heaven, above all outward works of charity, and are united and sunk in God, and God in them, so that between God and them time and our mortal state can interpose no means. When such are released from their bodies, in the same moment they enjoy their eternal blessedness. And they are not judged, but on the last day they shall with Christ give judgment upon other men. And then shall all mortal life and all temporal pain on earth and in purgatory have an end. And the damned shall sink and be swallowed up in the depths of hell, into a perdition and an everlasting terror without end, together with the devil and with his company. And in the twinkling of an eye, the blessed shall be in eternal glory with Christ their Bridegroom, and they shall see and taste and enjoy the inexhaustible riches of the Divine nature, eternally and evermore. This is the third coming of Christ, which we all attend, and which shall come to pass with all of us. The first coming, when God became man, and lived in humility and died in love for our sakes, this coming we ought to follow in our external works, with perfect habits of virtue, and in our hearts with charity and with careful humility. The second coming, which is now at hand, when He comes with grace into every loving heart, this coming we ought to covet, and to pray for each day, that we may persist and increase in new virtues. The third coming, to judgment or in the hour of our death, this coming we ought to await with longing, with trust and with piety, till we are released from this exile and come into the court of glories. This coming in these three manners is the second of the four principal matters.

PART THREE

'Go out'. Of the coming of virtue out of love and justness built upon humility (cap. xviii)

Now understand that Christ says at the beginning of His lesson 'See', that is, by means of charity and a pure conscience, as you heard at the beginning. Now He has shown us what we shall see, which is these three comings. Now He goes on to command what we should do, and says 'Go out'. If in you the first point is established, that you see in graces and in charity, and if you have properly observed Christ your monitor and how He went out, then out of charity and your loving scrutiny of your Bridegroom there will spring up in you a justness, so that you desire to follow Him in virtues. Then Christ says within you: Go out. This going out can be of three kinds. We may go out towards God, and towards ourselves, and towards our fellow-Christians, and this may be by means of charity and of justness and due proportion. For already charity makes its way up to the Kingdom of God, that is to God Himself, for He is the source from out of which charity immediately flowed, and in which, in the uniting of God and man, charity remains. Justness, which springs from charity, wishes to make perfect all the habits and all the virtues which are to the honour and profit of the Kingdom of God, that is the soul. These two, charity and justness, lay one foundation in the kingdom of the soul where God shall dwell, and this foundation is humility. These three virtues support all the weight and the building of all virtue and all excellence. For charity evermore holds man up before the inexhaustible goodness of God where it flows out, so that he may live to the honour of God, and persist and grow in all virtues and in righteous humility. And justness holds man up before the everlasting truth of God, so that he may discern the truth and be enlightened and achieve all virtues without straying. But still humility holds man up before the exalted power of God, so that he may ever remain poor and abased, and put his trust in God and think nothing of himself. This is the manner in which man should bear himself before God, so that he may ever grow in new virtue.

A. Humility as the Foundation and Mother of Virtues (*cap. xix*)

Now understand that because we have laid humility as our foundation, we shall speak of humility at the beginning. Humility is a quality of abasement or profundity: that is, an inward abasing or bowing down of the heart and of the mind before the exalted excellence of God. Righteousness commands and requires it, and, once the loving heart has charity, it cannot be forsaken. When the man who is humble and loving sees that God has so humbly served him, so lovingly and so faithfully, and that God is so mighty and so exalted and so excellent, and that man is so poor and so little and so base: from this there grows in the humble heart so great a reverence and worship towards God, for to pay honour towards God with all one's acts, interior and exterior, is the first and the most grateful of the deeds of humility, and the sweetest deed of charity, and the most needful work of righteousness. For the loving, humble heart cannot pay enough honour to God, nor to that which is excellent in His humanity, nor can it abase itself so low as it desires. And therefore it seems to the humble man that he must always remain in the service of God's honour and of humility. And he is humble and reverent before Holy Church and the sacraments, and he is moderate in eating and in drinking, in words, in making any reply, in his demeanour, in dress, in lowly service, in humble resignation without dissimulation and without affectation. And he is humble in what he practises, inwardly and outwardly, before

64

God and before all men, so that no-one because of him is offended. And thus he conquers and drives out pride, which is cause and beginning of all sins. Through humility are the traps of the devil and sin and the world broken open, and man is set in order within himself, and established within his own citadel of virtue, and heaven is opened to him, and God is inclined to him to hear his prayer; and he is filled full of graces, and Christ, that immovable Rock, is his foundation. He who there in his humility persists in virtue, he cannot err.

a. *Humility fosters obedience (cap. xx)*

Out of this humility comes obedience, for no-one but the humble man can be inwardly obedient. Obedience is a lowly, submissive, pliant disposition, and a ready willingness to perform all good things. Obedience makes man submissive to God's commandments and to His prohibitions and to His will. And it makes the senses and the sensual powers submissive to the *ratio superior*, so that man lives in ordered and rational fashion. And it makes man submissive and obedient to Holy Church, and to the sacraments, and to prelates and their teaching and commands and counsel, and to all the pious practices which men use in Christendom. It also makes man ready and submissive to all men in counsel, in deeds, in service, corporeal and spiritual, according to good judgment and to each one's needs. And it banishes disobedience, who is a daughter of pride more to be shunned than venom or poison. Obedience of will and of deeds is an adornment and a nourishment, manifesting man's humility. It makes peace in our converse one with another: if it is found in the bishop, as he has need that it be, it draws to him those that are subject to him; it maintains peace and equity among equals, and he who is obedient is beloved by those who owe him reverence and those who are above him, and he will be exalted by God and enriched with His gifts, which are eternal.

b. *Obedience fosters denial of our own will (cap. xxi)*

Out of this obedience comes a denial of our own will and our own self-esteem. For no-one is able to deny his own will in all things for the sake of another's will except the obedient man, even though one can perform external works and still follow one's own will. A denial of his own will makes a man to live without preference for this rather than that, in doing a thing or in letting it alone, in acting strangely or differently from the teachings and lives of the saints; but always in accordance with the honour and commandments of God, with the will of his bishop, and the quiet of all men with whom he is in communication, according to due discretion. Through denial of his own will in doing, in letting alone and in suffering, the stuff and the occasion of his pride are at once expelled, and his humility is made perfect in the highest grade. And God has power over man according to man's entire will, and man's will becomes so identical with God's will that man is unable to wish or to covet anything else. This man has then put out the old man, and has put on the new man, who is renewed and made according to God's dearest wish. Of such Christ says: 'Blessed are the poor in spirit',[1] that is, those who have denied their own will, 'for the Kingdom of heaven is theirs'.

c. *Denial of our own will fosters patience (cap. xxii)*

Out of the neglect of the will comes patience. For no-one may be perfectly patient in all things but he who has denied his own will for the will of God, and of all men in things profitable and opportune. Patience is a firm and quiet meekness under all things which can be sent by God or by His creatures to afflict a man. The patient man cannot be disturbed by any thing: not by the loss of earthly goods, of friends or of kinsmen, by sicknesses or disgrace, nor death nor life, nor purgatory nor devil nor hell. For he has entrusted himself to the will of God in righteous charity. Because he is never guilty of mortal

[1] St. Matthew v 3.

66

sin, it is therefore light for him, all that God ordains for him
in time and in eternity. With this patience man is also adorned,
and armed against fury and sudden anger and impatience in
suffering, which often disturb a man from within and from
without and make him prone to many kinds of temptation.

d. *Patience fosters meekness (cap. xxiii)*

Out of this patience come meekness and mercifulness. For
no-one but the patient man can be meek in adversity. Meekness
makes peace in man, and quiet undisturbed by any thing. The
meek man is well able to endure harsh words and harsh
treatment and harsh bearing and deeds and all injustice done
to him and to his friends, and still to be at peace, for meekness
is to suffer in peace. Because of meekness, man's capacity for
anger remains untouched in stillness, his capacity for envy is
exalted in virtues, the capacity for reason which perceives that
this is so is gladdened, and the conscience, which savours
this, remains in peace. For the second deadly sin, fury, anger
and wrath, is driven out by meekness, for the Spirit of God
rests in the humble, meek man, and Christ says: 'Blessed are
the meek, for they shall possess the earth',[1] that is, they shall
possess their own natures and earthly things in their stability
of heart.

e. *Meekness fosters mercifulness (cap. xxiv)*

Out of this same meekness grows mercifulness. For no-one
can be merciful, except the meek man. This mercifulness makes
a man to return loving bearing and courteous answers and all
works of mercy to those who are angry, for he hopes that they
may observe him and mend their ways. By means of gracious-
ness and mercifulness, charity remains alive and fruitful in
man. For the heart that is full of mercifulness is like to the
lamp full of precious oil: for the oil of mercifulness gives
light to erring sinners by good examples, and anoints and

[1] St Matthew v 4.

heals those that are bruised of heart and afflicted or enraged with words and deeds of comfort. And it burns and illumines those who are in virtue in the fire of charity, and it cannot be touched by dislike or ill-will.

f. *Mercifulness fosters compassion* (*cap. xxv*)

Out of mercifulness comes compassion and a common suffering with all men. For no man can suffer with all men, except he be merciful. This compassion is an inward stirring of the heart with pity for all men's need, material and spiritual. Compassion makes man to agonize and suffer with Christ in His sufferings, as man observes the cause of His torments, their manner, and His patience: His love, His wounds, His tenderness; His pain, His humiliation, His nobility; the wretchedness, the shame, the contempt, the crown, the nails; His mercifulness, and how He perished and died in meekness. This incomparable and manifold suffering of Christ our Redeemer and our Bridegroom stirs the merciful man to compassion and to pity for Christ. Compassion makes man to look upon himself, and to observe his faults and his lack of virtues and of care for God's honour; his lukewarmness and sloth and the multitude of his faults; how he has wasted time, and how now he lacks virtues and perfection. And this so causes man to have mercy upon himself in a just compassion. The next compassion makes man to see the erring and straying of men, their heedlessness of their God and of their eternal blessedness, their ingratitude for all the good that God has done to them, and all the suffering He has endured on their account. And that they are strangers to virtue, ignorant of it, unskilled in it; apt and servile to all wickedness and unrighteousness; how anxiously they scan the losing and the winning of earthly goods; how heedless and reckless they are of God and everlasting good and their eternal blessedness. And to observe this makes great compassion in a good man for the blessedness of all men. A man shall also in pity observe the material necessities of his fellow-Christian, and the manifold

68

sufferings of human nature. When a man observes men's hunger and thirst, cold, nakedness and sickness, poverty, rejection, the various oppressions of the poor, the sorrow that comes through the loss of kinsmen, of friends, of possessions, of honours, of peace, through the innumerable griefs that come upon human beings: all this moves a good man to compassion, and he suffers with all men. But his greatest suffering is that men are impatient under these afflictions and lose their reward, and often earn damnation. This is the work of compassion and mercifulness. This work of compassion and of love for all men conquers and drives out the third deadly sin, which is hatred and envy. For compassion is a piercing of the heart which love makes common to all men, and there is nothing that can heal it so long as any suffering remains in man: for God alone has pity on it and has complete knowledge of all suffering. And therefore Christ says: 'Blessed are those who mourn, for they shall be comforted.'[1] That shall be when in joy they reap that which now through compassion and sympathy they sow in sorrow.

g. *Compassion fosters mildness* (*cap. xxvi*)

Out of this pity comes mildness. For no-one can have the supernatural grace of mildness, with fidelity towards all men and with affection, save he who is pitiful, even if one is able to give with great mildness, but without charity and without the supernatural grace of mildness, individually to persons whom one favours. Mildness is a gentle outflowing of the heart that is stirred by charity and pity. When man with compassion observes the suffering and the Passion of Christ, out of this there springs mildness, which causes man to give to Christ, in return for His torments and His love, praise and thanks and honour and worship, and a joyful, humble servitude of soul and of body, in time and in eternity. When man with compassion and in pity for his own being looks upon himself, and on the good that God has done to him, and on his

[1] St. Matthew v 5.

defects, then man's heart must flow out to the mildness of God, His grace and fidelity and trustfulness, with a perfect and free will to serve Him evermore. A mild man, observing the folly and the error and the unrighteousness of men, yearns for God and prays to Him with inward trust, that He may cause His Divine gifts to flow, and may nurture His mildness in all men, till they acknowledge Him and turn themselves to the truth. This mild man also observes with compassion the bodily needs of all men: he serves them, he gives to them, he lends, he comforts each man according to his needs, according to his own ability and to discretion. By this mildness men are used to practise the seven works of mercy, the rich by their service and their possessions, the poor by good will and by just affection, which would make them do more if they had the means. Thus is the virtue of mildness made perfect. If in their depths they have mildness, all virtues are multiplied and all the powers of the soul are made lovely; for the mild man is always happy in spirit and carefree in heart, and overflowing in his yearning for God, and the merits of his virtuous works are free to all men. For the man who is mild and has no love for earthly things is ever the same in the eyes of God, however poor he may be: for all his inward life and all his feeling is an outflowing and a giving. And so he drives out the fourth deadly sin, avarice. Of such men Christ says: 'Blessed are the merciful, for they shall obtain mercy',[1] upon that day when they shall hear the voice say: 'Come, you blessed of my Father, inhabit the kingdom that is made ready for you through your mercifulness since the beginning of the world.'[2]

h. *Mildness fosters zeal for virtue (cap. xxvii)*

Out of this mildness grows a supernatural zeal, and a devotion to all virtues and to all propriety. No-one can experience zeal except a devout and mild man. This is an

---

[1] St. Matthew v 7.
[2] St. Matthew xxv 34.

inward, impatient passion to obtain all virtues and to be like to Christ and His saints. In this zeal a man longs, with heart and senses, soul and body and all that he is and all that he has and all that he may acquire, to make himself apt to the honour and the praise of God. This zeal makes a man to watch in recollection and in discretion and to perform deeds of virtue, corporeal and spiritual, in justness and due proportion. By means of this supernatural zeal all the powers of the soul are made manifest to God and ready for all virtues. The conscience is gladdened and the grace of God is multiplied; virtue is practised with delight and joy, and man's external works are made fair. The man who has obtained this living zeal from God, in him the fifth deadly sin is driven out, that is sloth of the mind and aversion from the virtues that may be of need. And at times this living zeal also drives out the heaviness and sloth of man's physical nature. Of these Christ says: 'Blessed are those who hunger and thirst for righteousness, for they shall be filled',[1] that is, when the glory of God shall be revealed to them, and shall fill each man according to the measure of his love and his righteousness.

i. *Zeal for virtue fosters moderation and sobriety* (*cap. xxviii*)

Out of this zeal comes moderation and sobriety, both interior and exterior. For no-one can well maintain a due measure of sobriety if he be not outstandingly devout and zealous to preserve soul and body in justness and due proportion. Sobriety preserves the *ratio superior* and the power of the senses from lack of moderation and over-enthusiasm: sobriety will neither taste nor know the things that are forbidden. The incomprehensible nature of God is beyond all creatures in heaven and in earth. For all that the creature comprehends is created. For God is above all creatures, and without and within all creatures. And all created comprehension is too narrow to comprehend Him. But if the creature is to comprehend God and understand and savour Him, then the creature

---

[1] St. Matthew v 6.

must be lifted above itself in God, and comprehend God in God. If anyone wished to know what God may be and to study to this purpose, that is forbidden to him: he would lose his wits. For behold, all created light is of no avail in knowing what God is: the quiddity of God is beyond all creatures. But He is that of which He gives evidence in nature and the scriptures and all creatures. We should believe in the articles of the creed, and not wish to know, for that is impossible so long as we are here on earth. This is sobriety. The hidden and profitable teaching of the scriptures, which the Holy Ghost has inspired, we should neither expound nor interpret, except through the lives of Christ and His saints. Man must observe nature and the scriptures and all creatures, and from that draw that which is profitable, and nothing more: that is sobriety of the spirit. Man must maintain sobriety in his senses, and he must control the power of the senses with reason, so that this power is not too much spent and wasted upon the savouring of food and drink, but so that he takes food and drink as a sick man takes a potion: as a necessary means of keeping his strength, with which to serve God. Man must be courteous and moderate in his words and deeds, in keeping silence and speaking, in eating and drinking, in doing a thing, in letting it alone, according to the custom of Holy Church and the example of the saints. By means of interior moderation and sobriety of the spirit a man maintains the strength and stability of his belief, the clarity of his understanding, the settled purpose of his reason to understand the truth, his aptness according to the will of God to all virtues, his peace of heart and unperturbed conscience: and through this he possesses a stable peace in God and in himself. And by means of exterior moderation and sobriety of the physical senses a man often maintains the health and stability of his physical being, his good repute in his communications with others, and his honourable name. And thus he is at peace with himself and with his fellow-Christians, because through moderation and sobriety he attracts and satisfies all men of good will, and he drives out the sixth deadly sin, which is immoderation, excess and gluttony. Of such men

Christ says: 'Blessed are the peaceable, for they shall be called the sons of God',[1] for they, like to the Son, have made peace in all creatures who desire it, and with those who make peace through moderation and sobriety, the Son shall share the inheritance of His Father: and that they shall possess with Him eternally.

k. *Sobriety fosters purity (cap. xxix)*

Out of this sobriety comes purity of soul and of body. For no-one may be perfectly pure in body and in soul except the man who is sober in body and in soul. Purity is that a man shall not cleave to any creature by the inclination of his pleasure, but only to God. For a man should commune with all creatures to his profit, but enjoy God alone. Purity of the spirit causes a man to cleave to God in a manner beyond the understanding and beyond the senses and beyond all the gifts which God can send into the soul. For then a creature wishes to forgo everything which he can receive through comprehension and feeling, and to rest in God. A man should not go to the sacrament of the altar for savour nor for desire, nor for delight nor peace nor for satisfaction, nor for sweetness nor for any other thing than for the honour of God and to increase in all virtues. This is purity of the spirit. Purity of the heart is that in every bodily temptation and stirring of nature man should of his free will turn to God with fresh confidence and without doubt, and in fresh trust and a firm desire evermore to remain with God. For to give consent to sin or to the delights which human nature desires as does a beast, that is to separate oneself from God. Purity of the body is that a man should keep and hold himself apart from immodest deeds, of whatever manner they may be, if conscience teaches and shows him that this would be immodesty, and contrary to the commandments and the honour and the will of God. Through these three kinds of purity is conquered and driven out the seventh deadly sin, which is a pleasurable aversion of the spirit from God towards

[1] St. Matthew v 9.

73

that which is created; and immodest physical deeds beyond
that which is permitted by Holy Church; and a dwelling of the
heart upon such physical pleasures as taste or the delight that
may be had in any creature, whatever it may be; I do not mean
those sudden stirrings of pleasure or delight which no man is
able to prevent.

Now you must know that the purity of the spirit preserves
man in his likeness to God, undisturbed by creatures, inclined
towards God and united with Him. Purity of body makes a
man like to the whiteness of the lily and the purity of the
angels: in resisting impurity, like to the redness of the rose and
the excellence of the martyrs: and because a man preserves
purity out of love and to the honour of God, so it is made
perfect, and so he is made like to the marigold, for this is one
of the fairest adornments of nature. Purity of heart causes
the grace of God to be renewed and increased. In the purity of
the heart all virtues are inspired and revealed and contemplated.
Purity preserves and guards the senses from without, and
compels and constrains the sensual delights from within; and
purity is an adornment of all man's interior life, and a lock to
close the heart against earthly things and against all deception,
and to open it to heavenly things and to all truth. And therefore
Christ says: 'Blessed are those who are pure of heart, for they
shall see God.'[1] In this seeing of God consists our eternal
joy and all our reward and the entrance to our blessedness.
Therefore a man must be sober and keep moderation in all
things, and hold himself aloof from society where there might
be any occasion whereby the purity of the soul or of the body
might be besmirched.

B. RIGHTEOUSNESS AS A WEAPON IN THE EXERCISE
OF VIRTUE (*cap. xxx*)

If now we wish to possess these virtues and to drive out
those vices which are opposed to them, then we must have

[1] St. Matthew v 8.

righteousness, and we must practise and contemplate this, until our death, in purity of heart. For we have three mighty adversaries who make trial of us and attack us at all times and in all places and in many manners. If we make peace with one of these three and are obedient to him, then we are conquered; for they act as one in drawing men into disorder. These three adversaries are the devil and the world and our own flesh, which last is the closest to us and often the most base and harmful. For our sensual delights are the weapons with which our foes make war upon us. Idleness of the spirit and lack of zeal for virtue and for the honour of God are the cause and occasion of battle, but the sickness of our human nature and our carelessness and ignorance of the truth are the sword with which sometimes our enemy will wound us and win this encounter. And it is for this reason that we must make a division within ourselves and take up sides, and we must hate and persecute and afflict with penances and with mortifications the lowest part of ourselves, which is animal, and fights against virtue in us, and wishes to depart from God: and this so that the animal part of us remains always suppressed and subjected to reason, and so that righteousness together with purity of heart always keep the upper hand in all virtuous works. And we shall gladly suffer all the troubling and suffering and persecution which God wishes to impose upon us through those who are opposed to virtue: this to the honour of God and to glorify suffering, and to obtain righteousness and to possess it in purity of heart. For Christ says 'Blessed are those who suffer persecution for the sake of righteousness, for the kingdom of heaven is theirs.'[1] For where righteousness is preserved in suffering and in virtuous works, that is the coin which weighs as much as the kingdom of God, and with which one obtains everlasting life. With this suffering a man goes out to God and to himself and to his fellow-Christians, in good living and in virtues and in every righteousness.

[1] St. Matthew v 10.

C. The soul as a kingdom over which the Beloved rules (*cap. xxxi*)

Whoever wishes to win and to keep these virtues, he must adorn and possess and rule over his soul as if it were a kingdom. Free will is king in the soul, which is itself by nature free and yet more free by grace. And it shall be crowned with a crown called charity. And the crown and the kingdom we shall receive, possess, rule and maintain from the emperor, who is lord and commander and king of kings. This king, free will, shall dwell in the highest city of the kingdom, which is the power of the soul to desire. And he shall be adorned and clad in a parti-coloured robe: on the right side with a Divine gift which is called fortitude, so that he may be strong and mighty to overcome every hindrance, and to sojourn in heaven in the palace of the supreme emperor, and in love to incline his crowned head before the King most high, upon Whom all his desire is centred: that is the proper work of charity, and in doing it a man adorns his crown, and doing that he receives his crown and maintains his kingdom and possesses it eternally. The left side of the robe shall be a cardinal virtue which is called moral fortitude. By that virtue shall free will, this king, suppress all immorality and foster all virtue, and possess in power his kingdom until the day of his death. This king shall appoint counsellors in his land, and they shall be the wisest of the land. The counsellors shall be these two Divine virtues, knowledge and discretion, illumined with the light of the grace of God. They shall dwell nearest to the king, in a palace which is called the reasoning power of the soul. And they shall be clad and adorned with a moral virtue called moderation, so that the king may always act, or refrain from acting, upon good counsel. By means of knowledge a man shall purge his conscience of all faults, and adorn it with all virtues: and with moderation a man shall give and take, shall do and let alone, be silent and speak, fast and eat, hear and answer, and act in all things according to knowledge and discretion, clad in a moral virtue which is called temperance or moderation.

This king, the free will, shall also establish in his kingdom a judge, who shall be righteousness. This is a Divine virtue, since it proceeds from love, and it is also the highest moral virtue. This judge shall dwell in the disposition, in the middle of the kingdom, in the power of the soul for anger. And he shall be adorned with a moral virtue called prudence. For righteousness cannot be perfect without prudence. This judge, righteousness, shall journey through the kingdom invested with the power and might of the king, and with the wisdom of the council, and with his own prudence. And he shall appoint and dismiss, judge and condemn, have power of life and death, maim, blind and make to see, raise up and cast down, and ordain all things in accordance with justice: and he shall scourge and chastise and deny every vice. The commoners of this kingdom, who are all the powers of the soul, shall be established in humility and in godly fear, submissive to God and to all virtues, each power according to its aptitude. He who thus possesses and guards the kingdom of his soul and has set it in order, he has gone out with love and virtue to God and to himself and to his fellow-Christian. This point is the third of the four principal matters.

PART FOUR

'To meet Him' (cap. xxxii)

WHEN a man sees by the grace of God, and has a pure conscience, and has observed the three comings of Christ our Bridegroom, and has gone out with virtues, there follows thereafter the meeting with our Bridegroom, and that is the fourth and the last point. In this meeting reposes all our blessedness, and the beginning and end of all virtues: and without this meeting no virtue will ever be achieved. Whoever wishes to meet with Christ as with his beloved Bridegroom, and wishes to dwell in Him and to live with Him for ever, he may now, in time, meet with Christ, and there are three points concerning this meeting and three manners of it. The first point is that he must be intent upon God in all things through which he shall earn eternal life. The second point is that he must not in this work be intent upon anything or love anything more than God or as much as God. The third point is that he shall rest in God with utmost devotion above all creatures and above all God's gifts and above all works of virtue and above all feeling which God may send to the soul and to the body.

A. THE FIRST WAY: A PURE INTENTION IN ALL THAT CONCERNS OUR BLESSEDNESS *(cap. xxxiii)*

Now understand: whoever shall be intent upon God must have God ever present with him, and present in His Divinity: that is to say that he must be intent upon Him Who is sole lord of heaven and earth and of all creatures: upon Him Who died for his sake, and can and will give him eternal blessedness. Whatever manner he uses, under whatever name he imagines

God, it shall be pleasing to Him. If he choose one Person of the Trinity as his image of the depth and the power of the Divine nature, it shall be pleasing to God. If he choose to contemplate God as saviour, redeemer, creator, master, blessedness, power, wisdom, truth, goodness, all of them attributes present to an immeasurable degree in the Divine nature, it shall be pleasing to God. For though God has many names which we ascribe to Him, His exalted nature is one and single, and to it His creatures can give no name. But because of His incomprehensible excellence and exaltedness we give all these names to Him, since we cannot know His name nor what He is.

This is the manner and the cognition which we must use to have God ever present with us in our intention. For to be intent upon God is to see God spiritually. Devotion, too, and love are necessary for this intention. For to recognize God and to see Him without love has no savour and neither helps nor profits man. This is why man must always be inclined towards God with love in all his deeds, God on Whom he is intent and Whom he loves above all things. This is to meet God in intention and in love. If the sinner is to turn from his sins with worthy penitence, he must meet God with contrition and of his free will, and with a just intention to serve God evermore and never again to commit sin. Then in this meeting he receives by the mercy of God a firm faith in eternal blessedness and in the forgiveness of his sins. And he receives the foundation of all virtue: faith, hope and love, and a joyful will to perform all virtues.

If a man is to advance in the light of belief and to contemplate all the works of Christ and all His sufferings and all that He has done and promised for us, and shall do until the day of judgment and into eternity, if a man is to contemplate this to the profit of his blessedness, he must meet Christ afresh and have Him ever present with him, yielding Him thanks and praise and worthy reverence for all His gifts and for all that He has done and will do into eternity. Then his faith will be strengthened, and he will be stirred more deeply and more

6

often to all virtues. If he is then to advance in virtuous works, he must also meet Christ with denying of himself, so that he do not seek for himself nor put forward any irrelevant reason for the meeting, but that he be discreet in all his works, and be intent upon God in all things, and upon His praise and His honour, and pursue that until his death. Then his reason will be enlightened and his charity increased, and he will be more devout and more apt to all virtues.

B. THE SECOND WAY. THE EXCLUSION OF ALL LOVE OR INTENTION TOWARDS THE CREATURE THAT MIGHT PUT IT NEXT TO GOD OR ABOVE HIM (*cap. xxxiv*)

A man shall be intent upon God in all good works: in evil works this is impossible. He must not have two objects to his intention, that is, he must not be intent upon God and add something else to that: but everything else that has a place in his intention shall be beneath God and not opposed to God, but it must promote God's honour and help and further man the better to come to God: and so it shall be well with man.

C. THE THIRD WAY. REST IN GOD ABOVE HIS CREATURES (*cap. xxxv*)

A man shall also rest upon Him and in Him Whom he loves and on Whom he is intent, more than upon all His messengers whom He sends, which are His gifts. The soul shall also rest in God above all the adornments and the presents which the soul can send by her messengers. The messengers of the soul are intentions, love and desire: these bring to God all good works and all virtuous living. Above all this the soul shall rest in her Beloved, above all multiplicity.

This is the fashion and the manner in which we shall meet Christ in all our life, and in all our works, and in all our virtues with just intention, so that we may meet Him in the hour of

our death in the light of glory. This manner and this fashion
as you have heard it described is called an active life. All men
have need of it, at least to ensure that their life is not contrary
to any virtue, even if they may not have all virtue in the active
life lived perfectly. For to live contrary to virtues is to live in
sin. For Christ says: 'The man who is not with Me is against
Me.'[1] The man who is not humble is arrogant: the man who is
arrogant and not humble does not belong to God. And so it
is with respect to all sins and all virtues: man must always have
virtue and be in a state of grace, or be the opposite, and be
in sin. Let each man scrutinize himself, and let him live as is
shown here.

D. THE TRANSIT FROM THE ACTIVE LIFE TO THE LIFE OF YEARNING FOR GOD (*cap. xxxvi*)

The man who thus lives in this perfection as it is shown here,
and offers up all his life and all his deeds to the honour and
the praise of God, and is intent upon God and loves God
above all things, he will often be touched by a desire to see,
to know, to understand what is the nature of this Bridegroom,
Christ, Who became man for his sake and laboured in love
until His death, and has banished his sins and the devil, and
has brought home to man Himself and His grace, and has
bequeathed him His sacraments, and has promised him His
kingdom and Himself as an eternal reward: and has given him
living desire, fervent faith, sweetness and innumerable gifts
in every fashion in which man has need of them. When such
a man contemplates all this, he is moved beyond all measure
with desire to see Christ his Bridegroom, and to understand
what is His own interior nature: though he understands Him
in His works, that seems to him not to be enough. Then he
must do as Zacchaeus the publican did, who wished to see
what Christ was like.[2] He must run faster than all the crowds,

---

[1] St. Luke xi 23.
[2] St. Luke xix 1–10.

who are the multitudes of God's creatures, who make us little and low, so that we cannot look at God. And he must climb up the tree of faith, which grows downwards from above, for its roots grow in the Godhead. This tree has twelve branches, which are the twelve articles of our creed. The lowest speak of the humanity of God, and of the matters which are needful to our blessedness in soul and in body. The highest branches of this tree tell of the Godhead, of the Trinity of the Persons and of the unity of the natures of God. And this man must hold fast to this unity at the top of the tree, for it is there that Christ must needs pass by with all His gifts.

Jesus comes this way, and He sees the man, and He speaks to him in the light of faith: He tells him that in His Divinity He is immeasurable and incomprehensible, unattainable and unfathomable, exalted far above all created light and all finite understanding. That is the highest recognition of God which man can have in the active life: that he should recognize in the light of faith that God is beyond comprehension and cognition. In this light Christ says to man's desire: 'Go down quickly, because today I need to dwell in thy house.'[1] This hasty going down is nothing else but the soul's flowing down with desire and love into the depths of the Godhead which no understanding can touch in created light. But desire and love go in where understanding is not admitted. When the soul thus inclines herself with love and with intent towards God, beyond that which she understands, then in this she rests and dwells in God, and God in her. When the soul with desire climbs up above the multitude of creatures and above the work of the senses, and above the light of nature, then she meets with Christ in the light of faith. And she is enlightened, and she recognizes that God is unrecognizable and incomprehensible. When she in desire inclines towards this incomprehensible God, then she meets with Christ and is filled full of His gifts. When she loves and rests above all gifts and above herself and above all creatures, then she dwells in God and God in her. That is how we shall meet Christ in the highest

[1] St. Luke xix 5.

form of the active life. If you have justness in charity, and have laid down humility as your foundation, and if upon that you have established a dwelling, which is the virtues which are shown here; and if you have met Christ with praise, with intention and with love, so you dwell in God and God dwells in you, and you have made the active life your own. And this is the first life of which we wished to speak.

BOOK TWO

THE LIFE OF YEARNING
FOR GOD

THE prudent virgin, that is, a pure soul, who has abandoned earthly things and lives with God in virtues, she has taken into the vessel of her heart the oil of charity and virtuous works, by the light of the lamp which is an unsullied conscience; but when Christ the Bridegroom tarries in trust and in fresh inpouring of gifts, the soul becomes sleepy and weary and slumbers. In the middle of the night, that is when men least expect it and watch for it, a cry is raised in the soul, a cry not of the senses: 'See, the Bridegroom comes: go out to meet Him.' Of this seeing, and of an inward coming of Christ, and of a spiritual going out of man to the meeting with Christ, of all this let us speak, and let us expound and make plain these four matters as they concern an inward exercise of yearning, which many achieve through the life of virtue and through interior devotion. In these words Christ teaches us four things. First, He wishes our understanding to be enlightened with a supernatural light. We observe that from the word which He employs: 'See'. Next, He shows us what it is needful for us to see, that is, the inward coming of our Bridegroom, the eternal truth. We understand that when He says 'The Bridegroom comes'. Thirdly, He commands us to go out in inward exercise according to justness and due proportion, and therefore He says 'Go out'. Fourthly, He shows us the end and the reason of all this labour, which is our meeting, in a unity of the Godhead delectable to the soul, with Christ our Bridegroom.

PART ONE

'See.' The foundation of the life of yearning for God

A. The three conditions for seeing (*cap. i*)

Let us now consider the first matter. Christ says 'See'. So that we may see supernaturally in our interior exercise, three points are needful. The first is the light of the grace of God, in a manner higher than one can experience it in an exterior, active life without an inward zeal. The second point is that one must make one's mind bare of alien images and one's heart free of cares, so that one may be free and not distracted by images, and unfettered and empty of all creatures. The third point is that, untroubled by all inordinate affections, one should freely turn one's will, with a gathering together of all one's strengths, bodily and spiritual, so that there is a flowing into the unity of God and into the unity of the spirit, so that the rational creature may attain to the high unity of God and may possess it supernaturally. For this reason has God created heaven and earth and all things, and for this reason did He become man, and taught us and lived for us, and Himself showed the way to this unity. And He died in the bond of love, and He ascended, and He has unbarred for us that same unity, where we with Him may possess everlasting blessedness.

B. Of the three unities which are in us by nature (*cap. ii*)

Now observe carefully: we find in all men a threefold unity, naturally, and supernaturally in good men.

a. *The three unities and their natural properties (cap. iii)*

The first and the highest unity is in God: for all creatures depend upon this unity for their being and life and preservation, and should they separate themselves in this manner from God, they fall into nothing and become nothing. This unity is by nature in our very being, whether we are good or bad, and without our co-operation it does not make us either holy or blessed. We possess this unity in ourselves, and yet beyond ourselves, as a beginning and a preservation of our being and our life. There is also another union or unity in us by nature, that is a unity of our superior powers, from which unity operatively they derive their natural source: in unity of the spirit or of the mind. This is the same unity which depends upon God, but here man has it operatively, and there essentially; yet the spirit is still entire in each unity, according to the totality of its substance. We possess this unity in ourselves above our powers of sense; and from this come memory and understanding and will and all the power of spiritual acts. It is in this unity that one calls the soul 'spirit'. The third unity which is in us by nature is our possession of physical strength in the unity of the heart, beginning and source of physical life. The soul possesses this unity in the life and the vitality of the heart; and from here flow all physical acts and the five senses. And because of this the soul is called 'soul', because the soul is the form of the life, and animates the body, that is, the soul makes the body living and preserves it living. These three unions exist naturally in man, as one life and one realm. In the lowest, man is sensual and animal; in the middle union, man is rational and spiritual; in the highest, man is preserved in his essence. And this exists naturally in all men.

b. *The three unities and their supernatural possession in the active life (cap. iv)*

Now these three unities, as it were as a realm and an everlasting dwelling-place, are supernaturally adorned and possessed with moral virtues in charity, and with the active life. And they are still better adorned and more honourably possessed with interior exercises, added to the active life. The lowest unity, which is physical, is supernaturally adorned and possessed with exterior exercises performed in moral perfection according to the manner of Christ and of His saints; and adorned by bearing Christ's cross with Him, and mortifying nature according to the commands of Holy Church and the teaching of the saints, discreetly and according to one's natural strength. The second unity, which is in the spirit and pre-eminently spiritual, is adorned and supernaturally possessed with the three Divine virtues of faith, hope and love, and with the inflowing of God's graces and gifts, and with willing inclination towards all virtues, so as to follow the example of Christ and of Christendom. The third and the highest unity is above our intellectual comprehension, and yet exists essentially within us. It is supernaturally possessed by us when in all our acts of virtue we intend God's praise and honour, and rest in Him, beyond all intention and beyond ourselves and beyond all things. It is from this unity that we have drifted away, because we are creatures: and essentially we have remained within it; and by means of charity, in loving we return again into it. Such are the virtues which adorn these three unities in the active life.

c. *The preparation for the supernatural properties in the life of yearning for God (cap. v)*

Now let us go on to speak of how these three unities are more highly adorned and more honourably possessed with interior exercises, added to the active life. When a man by means of charity and an intention towards God offers himself up to God in all his works and in all his living, to His honour and praise, and seeks rest in God beyond all things, then he must, with humility and patience and forgetfulness of himself, still await new riches and new gifts, with certain confidence: and still he must be untroubled, whether God gives to him or does not give. Thus a man makes himself ready and pleasing, so that he may receive the interior life of yearning for God. When the vessel is prepared, one pours into it the precious liquor. There is no more precious vessel than the loving soul, nor is there a more cordial drink than the grace of God. Thus shall man offer up to God all his works and all his life with a single intention towards God, and he shall rest, beyond intention, and beyond himself, and beyond all things, in the high unity where, without any mean, God and the loving spirit are united.

C. THE ENLIGHTENMENT IN THE HIGHEST UNITY (*cap. vi*)

Out of this unity in which the spirit is, without any mean, united with God, from out of this flow grace and all gifts. Out of this same unity where the spirit rests beyond itself in God, Christ the everlasting truth says: 'See, the Bridegroom comes: go out to meet Him.' It is Christ, Who is the light of truth, Who says 'See'. For through Him do we come to see, because He is the light of the Father, and without Him there is no light in heaven or in earth. This speaking of Christ within us is nothing else than an inflowing of His light and of His grace. This grace falls upon us in the unity of our superior powers and of our spirit, where the highest powers flow out operatively in all virtues through the power of grace, and return again into the same being in the bond of love. In this unity reposes the power and the beginning and the end of all deeds of the creature, natural and supernatural, in so far as such deeds are performed in manner of the creature, through grace and Divine gifts and the power of the creature. And therefore God gives His grace in the unity of the superior powers, so that man may always perform works of virtue through the power and riches and compulsion of grace. For He gives grace for the sake of works, and Himself, Who is above all grace, for the sake of the soul's delectation and rest. The unity of our spirit is our dwelling in Divine peace and in the wealth of charity: and the virtues in all their multiplicity enclose themselves therein, and live in the singleness of the spirit. Now the grace of God, which flows out from God, is an inward compulsion or driving of the Holy Ghost, Who from within us drives our spirit and incites it in all virtues. This grace flows from within, not from without. For God is more truly within us than are we ourselves, and His inward driving or working in us, natural or supernatural, is more within us and closer to us than are our own works; and therefore God works in us from within outwards, and all creatures work from without inwards. And because of this, grace and all Divine gifts and God's inward speaking come from within, in the unity of our spirit, not from without in the imagination by means of sensual images.

D. The conditions for receiving enlightenment
(cap. vii)

So then Christ says spiritually within the man devoted to Him: 'See'. Three matters, as I said before, make man to see in his interior exercises. The first is the shining in on him of the grace of God. The grace of God in the soul is like to the candle in the lantern or in a vessel of glass: for it gives warmth and light and shines through the vessel, which is the good man. And grace manifests itself to the man who has it within him, if he is zealous in scrutinizing himself; and it manifests itself also through him to other men, in virtues and in good examples. The inward shining of the grace of God stirs and moves a man inwardly, from within him, suddenly, and that swift stirring is the first point that makes us to see. Out of this swift stirring by God comes the second point, achieved by man, that is, a gathering together of all his powers, from within and from without, in unity of the spirit and in the bond of love. The third point is freedom, that man is able to go within himself, unhindered by any sensual image or other obstacle, as deeply as he will and as it seems to him to be for his own good. That is to say that man be unimpeded by earthly love and sorrow, by gain and by loss; by exaltation and by depression; by the cares of others; by joy and by misery; and that he be not preoccupied with any creature. These three points make man to see in his inward exercises. If you have achieved these three, you have a foundation and a beginning of interior exercise and of the interior life.

PARTS TWO AND THREE

'The Bridegroom comes, go out': The threefold coming of Christ, and our response (cap. viii)

EVEN if the eyes were clear and the sight keen, and they were
to reflect the loveable and gladdening object, to see clearly
would enable and advance not at all, or little. And for this
reason Christ shows to the enlightened and understanding
eyes what it is that they should see, that is the inward coming
of Christ their Bridegroom. One finds three manners of
special coming in men who exercise themselves with devotions
in the interior life. And each of the three comings raises man
into an exalted state of being, and into interior exercises.
The first coming of Christ in interior exercise compels and
drives man sensibly from within, and draws man with all
strength upwards to heaven, and urges him to have unity
with God. Man feels this driving and this drawing in his
heart and in the unity of all his bodily powers, and particularly
in his capacity for desire. For this coming touches and moves
man in his lowest nature, for that nature must at this time
be purged and adorned and enkindled and drawn in. This
driving of God from within both gives and takes: it enriches
and impoverishes, it makes men prosperous and destitute,
it causes them to hope and despair, it heats and chills.
The gifts and the acts that come through this in opposition
to one another are not to be told by any tongue. This
coming by way of exercises divides itself in four manners,
each one higher than the next, as we shall hereafter show.
And through this in his interior life man's lowest nature is
adorned.

The second manner of the inward coming of Christ, in
great excellence and in likeness to Him Himself, and

in greater gifts and illumination, is a flowing-in of the riches of Divine gifts into the highest power of the soul, and these gifts make the spirit stable, and illuminate it, and make it rich in diverse fashions. This flowing-in of God demands a flowing-out and a flowing back again, with all richness, into the same depths from which the flowing comes out. In this flowing God gives, and God shows wonders. But He demands all His gifts back again from the soul, multiplied, above any measure that His creature can afford. This exercise and this existence are more excellent and more like to God than is the first, and through this the three superior powers of the soul are adorned.

The third manner of the inward coming of Our Lord is an inward stirring or touching in the unity of the spirit, where the highest powers of the soul have their dwelling and flow out and come back again and always remain within, one and single, by means of the bond of love and the unity of the spirit according to nature. This coming makes the most inward and the highest existence in the interior life. And through this the unity of the spirit is adorned in diverse fashions.

Now Christ at each of His comings demands from us a special going-out of ourselves, in our entire life, according to the manner of His coming. And therefore at each coming He says spiritually in our hearts: 'Go out in your life and in your exercise, in the manner in which My grace and My gifts compel you.' For according to the manner in which the Spirit of God drives and compels and draws and flows in and touches us, so we must go out and so we must fare, if we are to become perfect. But if we resist the Spirit of God with a life unlike to Him, we lose that inward compulsion, and then virtue must remain strange to us. These are the three comings of Christ in interior exercise. Now let us explain and make clear each coming separately. And observe with diligence and care, for whoever has not felt this shall not easily understand it.

A. The fourfold manner of the first coming in man's heart

a. *The first manner. The sensible enkindling and consolation (cap. ix)*

The first coming of Christ in the exercise of yearning is an inwardly felt compulsion of the Holy Ghost, which stimulates and compels us towards all virtues.

1. *The rising sun upon the mountains*

Let us liken this coming to the shining and the power of the sun, which in the twinkling of an eye, after it has risen, illumines and transfuses and warms all the world. In just the same manner Christ, the everlasting Sun, Who dwells in the highest part of the spirit, breaks forth and shines and illumines: and He illumines and enkindles the lowest part of man, which is the heart in his body and his sensual powers, and this happens in less time than the twinkling of an eye, for God's working is swift. But he to whom this shall happen must see inwardly with understanding eyes. The sun shines in the mountainous country in the middle of the world upon the mountain ranges, and brings summer there early, and makes the fruits good and the wine strong and the land to be full of joy. The same sun gives its light to the low countries in the outermost part of the world. The climate is colder and the power of the sun's heat less. Still the sun brings forth much good fruit there, but in those parts one finds little wine. The men who live in the lowest part of themselves, governed by their bodily senses, and yet with good intention in virtuous living and with external devotions and in the grace of God, they bring forth much good fruit of virtues in many fashions.

But they feel little of the wine of inward joy and spiritual comfort. The man who now will feel the shining of the everlasting sun which is Christ Himself must see, and dwell in the high lands upon the mountain, with a gathering together of all his powers, and he must be lifted up with all his heart to God, free and untroubled by love or woe or by any creature.

There Christ, the Sun of Righteousness, shines in the heart that is free and lifted up: and those are the mountains which I mean.

2. *The coming*

Christ, that glorious Sun and that Divine Radiance, in His inward coming illumines and transfuses and enkindles in the might of His Spirit the free heart and all the powers of the soul. And this is the first work of the inward coming in the exercise of yearning. Just as the power and the nature of fire enkindles the substance that is prepared for fire, so Christ enkindles the heart that is ready and free and lifted up with the inward heat of His inward coming. And in this coming He says: 'Go out in exercises according to the manner of this coming.'

3. *The effect of the coming, and our response*

Out of this heat comes singleness of the heart. For we cannot attain to true singleness, unless the Spirit of God kindle His fire in our hearts. For fire makes all things which it may overpower and transform into one, like to it. Singleness is that man feel himself gathered together from within with all his powers in the singleness of his heart. Singleness makes the heart's inward peace and rest. Singleness of the heart is a bond, drawing together and binding up body and soul, heart and sense and all man's powers from without and from within, in the singleness of love.

Out of this singleness comes inwardness. For no man is able to attain inwardness if he be not singly gathered together in himself. Inwardness is that a man inwardly be turned from within to behold his own heart, so that he is able to understand, and be able to feel the working or the speaking of God within him. Inwardness is a sensible fire of love which the Spirit of God has kindled and causes to burn. Inwardness burns man and compels and stimulates him from within, and he does not know whence this has come or what has happened to him.

Out of inwardness comes sensible love, which goes through

and through the heart of man and the capacity of the soul for yearning. No man may have this yearning love with its sensible savour in the heart unless in his thoughts he be inward. Sensible love and loving is a yearning, well-savouring delight which man has in God, as if in some eternal good in which all good is comprehended. Sensible love is at the bidding of all creatures in the measure of their delight, not of their need. Inward love feels itself touched from within by an everlasting loving which love must foster. Inward love denies and despises lightly all earthly things, so that it may attain that on which its loving is set.

Out of this sensible love comes devotion to God and to His honour. For no-one can have yearning devotion in his heart except the man who bears within himself this sensible love towards God. Devotion is as if the fire of love and of loving sent up its flames of yearning to heaven. Devotion touches and stimulates man to the service of God from without and from within. Devotion makes man's body and soul to flourish in honour and worship before God and before all men. Devotion is demanded of us by God in all the services which we shall perform for Him. Devotion purges body and soul of all those earthly things which can let and hinder. Devotion instructs and gives us the true way of blessedness.

Out of this inward devotion comes thankfulness. For no-one can thank and praise God so well as the man who is inwardly devout. Truly we ought to thank and praise God, for He created us creatures of understanding, and He ordered and put to our service heaven and earth and the angels: and for that He became man because of our sins; and for that He taught and instructed us through His life, and in the habit of humility was our servant, and suffered a shameful death for us, and has promised His eternal kingdom and Himself for our reward and also for our deserving. And that He has spared us in our sins, and yet thereafter is willing to forgive us or has forgiven us, and has poured His grace and His love into our soul. And that He wishes evermore to dwell and to remain in us and with us. And that He will sustain us and has sustained us according to all our needs all the days of our life with His most excellent sacraments. And that He has bequeathed to us His body and His blood for meat and drink according as each man through yearning hungers and thirsts for Him. And that He has set up before us nature and the scriptures and all creatures as exemplar and mirror, so that we may observe and learn how in all our works we should walk in the way of virtues. And that He has granted us health, strength and power, and at other times sickness, for our profit, and has contrived for us the lack of outward things, and inward peace and rest. And that we bear the name of Christians, and are born of Christian folk. For all this we should thank God here, so that we may there on high thank Him for evermore.

And we should also praise God with all of which we are capable. To praise God is that man in all his life should offer to the Divine Power honour and reverence and worship. To praise God is the work nearest and most proper to the angels and saints in the kingdom of heaven, and to the men upon earth who love God. Man should praise God with his heart, with his desire, with his uttermost strength: with words, with deeds; with body, with soul and with possessions, in humble service, interior and exterior. Those who do not praise God here shall remain everlastingly dumb. To praise God is for the loving heart the most gratifying and delectable deed. The heart which is full of praise desires that all creatures should praise God. There is no end to praising God, for that is our blessedness: and truly we shall praise Him to all eternity.

Out of inward thanks and praise there comes a two-fold woe in the heart, and a torment in yearning. The first woe is because we fall short in our thanks and praise and honour, and in the service of God. The second is because we do not grow as we desire in charity, in virtue, in trust, in perfect living, so that we might be worthy to thank God and to praise Him and to serve Him as we should. This is the second woe. These are both root and fruit, beginning and end of all inward virtues. The inward pain and woe we have because we fall short in virtue and in the praise of God is the highest work in this first manner of interior exercise, and through this work the exercise is brought to perfection.

4. *A similitude of the boiling water*

Now observe this similitude of how the exercise ought to be. When natural fire by means of its heat and power has driven water or other liquid until it boils, that is its highest work: then the water turns and falls back again into the same depth, and is then driven up again by the same action by the power of the fire, so that the fire is always driving and the water is always boiling. The inward fire of the Holy Ghost works in just the same manner: it compels and stimulates and drives the heart and all the strength of the soul to boiling-point: that is, to thank God and to praise Him in the manner that I have said before. And so too one falls back again into the same depth, where the Spirit of God burns, so that the fire of love be ever burning, and the heart of man be ever yielding thanks and praise, with words and with deeds, and remain ever lowly: that man pay great heed to what he should do and would gladly do, and little heed to what he has achieved.

5. *The most sublime part of this manner: the ascending sun in spring*

So when the summer is near and the sun is high, the earth's humidity is drawn up, first through the roots and then through the trunk into the branches of the tree; and from this come leaf and blossom and fruit. When Christ, the eternal Sun, mounts high and ascends in our hearts, so that summer comes there and they are made fair in virtues, in just the same manner He gives light and His heat in our yearning, and draws the heart away from all multiplicity of earthly things, and makes singleness and inwardness, and causes the heart to swell and to put forth leaves with inward love, and to flower with a yearning devotion, and to bring forth fruit with thanks and with praise, and to keep the fruit forever, in humble sorrow because it is not more. Here in this you have the first manner of interior exercise, of the four principal manners which adorn the lowest part of man.

b. *Second manner: the excess of consolation (cap. x)*

But since we have likened the four manners of the coming of Christ to the shining and the power of the sun, we may find other such virtues and action of the sun which causes the fruit to hasten and to multiply.

1. *The sun in Gemini*

As the sun mounts towards its zenith and comes into Gemini, which is as much as to say a thing which is twofold but of one nature, in the middle of May, it then has double power in trees and in herbs and in all things that grow in the earth. When then the planets which govern nature are well disposed, as the season of the year requires, the sun shines upon the earth and draws its humidity up into the air. From this come the dew and rain, and the fruit grows, and is greatly multiplied. So in the same fashion when Christ the bright Sun mounts in our hearts above all things, and when the demands of our bodily nature, which are in opposition to the spirit, are well subdued and disposed through discretion, and the virtues have their place in us according to the fashion you heard when we spoke of the first manner, and when through the heat of charity all the savour and all the rest that man experienced in virtues is offered and elevated to God with thanks and with praise: from this at times comes a sweet rain of new inward consolation, and a heavenly dew of divine sweetness. This makes every virtue to grow and to double itself in twofold fashion.

2. *The coming*

This is a new and special working and a new coming of Christ in the loving heart, and through this, man is exalted into a higher form of being than he had before. In this sweetness, Christ says: 'Go out in the manner of this coming.'

3. *The effect of the coming*

Out of this sweetness comes a richness of the heart and of all the bodily powers, so that it seems to man that he be caught up from within by a Divine embrace in love. This richness and this consolation are greater and more satisfying in the soul and in the body than could be all the riches that the earth might yield, even if one man could possess them all. In this richness God through His gifts sinks Himself in the heart of man, with so much consolation savouring well and so much joy that the heart from within overflows. This makes man to see how wretched they are who dwell without love. A man is rich since his heart flows away, and he cannot restrain himself for his fullness of inward joy.

Out of these riches comes a spiritual drunkenness. Spiritual drunkenness is that a man receives more sensible savour and richness than his heart or his desire can covet or hold. Spiritual drunkenness makes a man to behave in many strange ways. Some such men drunkenness makes to sing and to praise God out of their fullness of joy. And some such man it makes to weep great tears, out of the richness of his heart. To some such man it sends violence into every limb, so that he must needs run, jump, skip. Another this drunkenness so overwhelms that he must clap with his hands and exult. One such will cry out with a loud voice, and show the fullness that he feels within him. Another must needs be silent, and melt for richness in his every sense. Sometimes it seems to such a man that all the world has felt this that he feels. At times it seems to him that no-one has tasted this where he is now touched. Many a time it seems to him that he never can, never will lose this richness. Sometimes he is astonished that all men do not become godly. Sometimes it seems to him that God alone is everything to him, and to no-one as much as to him. Sometimes he is astonished to know what this richness may be, or whence it comes, or what has happened to him. This is the richest life in manner of physical sensation that any man can attain upon this earth. Sometimes these riches become so great that it seems to man that his heart must burst with all these manifold gifts and wondrous works.

4. *Our response, and the obstacles we meet*

So man must honour and praise with humble heart the Lord Who is able to do all this, and thank Him with inward devotion because He will do it; and always man must observe in his heart and say with his mouth with true intention: 'Lord, I am not worthy of this, but I have indeed need of Thine inexhaustible goodness and that Thou shouldst preserve me.'[1] In this humility he may grow and increase in higher virtues.

When now this coming and this manner are granted to such men at the beginning when they turn away from the world, provided that they make a complete conversion, and renounce all the consolations of the world so that they exist and live entirely for God, even so they are still tender, and have need of milk and sweet things, not of strong meat, great temptations and to be abandoned by God. Frost and mist hinder much these men at these times, for this comes just in the middle of May according to the seasons of the interior life. Frost is their will to be something, or their belief that they are something, or their opinion in some respect of themselves, or that they may have earned consolation or are worthy of it. That is frost, which would deprive blossom and fruit of all virtue. Mist is when a man wishes to rest upon inward consolation and on sweetness: that makes the air of the reason dark and the powers wither which should be opened out and blossom and bring fruit. And because of this man loses his recognition of the truth. Nevertheless a man will cling to false sweetness at such a time: and this comes from the devil, who to this end seduces man.

5. *A similitude of the bee*

I wish to describe a short similitude to you, so that you do not err, but govern yourselves well in this way of life. So you should observe the wise bee, and do as she does. She lives in unity in the company of her fellows, and goes out, not in the storm but in calm, settled weather, in the sunshine, to search for all the flowers in which sweetness is to be found. She settles

[1] Cf. St. Matthew viii 8, and the prayer before the priest's communion in the Canon of the Mass.

not upon any one flower, nor on any one sweetness nor beauty. But she draws out from them honey and wax, which is sweetness and the means to illumination, and she returns to the unity of her companions, so that she may become fruitful to their great profit. The heart that is plundered as the bee robs the flower, and into which Christ the everlasting Sun does shine, He causes to swell and bloom and flow, and all its inward powers, with joy and with sweetness. So should the wise man do as the bee does, and should fly with care and reason and discretion to all the gifts and all the sweetness that ever he experienced, and to all the good that God ever did to him; and with the sting of charity and inward care should test all the multiplicity of consolation and richness, and not rest upon any one of the flowers of God's gifts; but, heavy-laden with thankfulness and praise, fly back again into that unity in which he desires to rest and dwell with God eternally. This is the second manner of interior exercise which adorns the lowest part of man in many fashions.

c. *Third manner: of the power of our ascent to God (cap. xi)*

1. *The sun in Cancer*

When the sun has mounted as high in the heavens as it is able, that is to say into Cancer, so that it cannot go any higher, but now begins to decline, then its heat is greater than at any other time of the year, and the sun draws up all the humidity so that the earth becomes most dry and the fruit most ripe. In just the same fashion, when Christ the Divine Sun is exalted as high as may be in our hearts, that is to say above all gifts and consolation and sweetness that we are able to receive from Him, so that we do not rest upon any sensation which God is able to pour into our souls, however great it may be, if we are masters of ourselves, but so that we always turn inward again, as has been shown before, with humble praise and inward thanks, to the same depths whence all gifts flow out according to the need and the worth of God's creatures: then Christ is exalted into the highest place in our hearts, and wishes to draw all things to Him: and these things are all our powers. When neither sensation nor consolation can conquer or hinder the loving heart, which is willing to forgo all consolations and all gifts so that it may find Him Whom it loves, from this springs the third manner of interior exercise, by which man is exalted and adorned in his affections and in the lowest part of himself.

2. *The coming*

The first work of Christ and the beginning of this manner is that God draws up towards heaven the heart and the desire and all the powers of the soul, and demands that they be united with Him, and says spiritually in the heart: 'Go out of yourselves to Me, in the manner in which I draw you and command you.' I cannot well demonstrate this drawing and this commanding to rude, insensitive men. But it is an inward need and command in the heart that it should go out towards a higher unity. This inward need is satisfying to the heart beyond all things which it ever felt. For from this springs a new manner and a higher exercise.

3. *The effect, and our response*

Here the heart plunders itself in joy and desire, and all its veins are open, and all the powers of the soul are ready and desirous to bring that to pass which is there demanded of the heart by God and His unity. This need is the shining-in of Christ the eternal Sun, and it makes so great a satisfaction and joy in the heart, and makes the heart to open itself so wide to Him, that it can hardly be withered away. Because of this man is wounded in his heart from within, and feels the wounding of love. To be wounded by love is the sweetest sensation and the most grievous pain that man can bear. To be wounded by love is a sure token that one shall be healed. The wound of the spirit brings with it well and woe at the same time. Christ the very Sun breaks forth and shines again into the wounded open heart, and demands unity anew. This renews the wound and all the wounding.

This inward demand and this need, and God's creature's

raising up of himself and waiting, ready, with all the power that he can command, but without ever being able to touch or attain unity, this causes a torment of the spirit: just as the innermost place in the heart and the source of life is wounded by love, and as man cannot attain to that which he desires above all else, and must ever remain there where he does not wish to be: so out of these two comes the torment. Here Christ has gone up into the highest place in the mind, and casts down His Divine rays into the yearning depths and the desire of the heart: and His shining burns and dries and uses up all the humidity, which is the strength and power of man's nature. The desirous open heart and the shining in of the Divine rays make a lasting torment. When man can neither attain to God nor forgo Him, out of these two spring a tempest and an impatience in such a man, from without and from within. For in the time that man is tempest-tossed, no creature can be of avail to him, to bring him rest nor to achieve anything for him in heaven or on earth. At such times in this tempest are given to him from within and enunciated great and profitable words and rare teachings and wisdom. In this tempest within man, he is ready to suffer all that he can suffer, so that he may achieve that which he loves. The tempest of love is an inward impatience, that under no compulsion will use or follow reason if man do not attain to that which he loves. This inward tempest devours man's heart and drinks his blood. Now is the sensible inward heat greater than in all the rest of man's life; and man's physical nature is secretly wounded and withered without any action from without: and the fruit of virtues hastens to ripening more than in any of the manners that have been shown before.

At this same time of the year the natural sun runs into the house of Leo, who has a cruel nature, because he is lord over all the beasts. In just the same way, when man enters into this manner of being, then Christ the bright Sun stands in Leo. For the rays of His heat are so hot that the heart's blood boils in the tempestuous man. And this tempestuous manner, so long as it lasts, masters and overpowers all other manners, for it wishes to be free of manner, that is to say without any fashion. Sometimes the tempestuous man falls into a yearning and an impatient desire to be released from the prison of his body, so that he may be united with Him Whom he loves. So he casts up the eyes of his spirit and beholds the heavenly hall of glory and joy, and sees his Love there crowned within, flowing out in plenteous riches into His saints: and he must be deprived of this. From this sometimes in such a man come bodily tears and a great longing. Then he looks down and observes this land of exile in which he is imprisoned and from which he may not depart: and so his tears flow in affliction and lamentation. This natural weeping is able to settle and cool a man, and it is beneficial to his physical nature, enabling it to retain its power and might, and him to endure this tempestuous manner. There are many kinds of care and exercise with manner which are beneficial to the tempestuous man, enabling him to retain his strength and to live long in virtues.

Out of this tempest and impatience such men are sometimes drawn up in the spirit above their senses, and some truth is spoken to them with words, or shown to them in images or likenesses, which is needful to them or to other men or to the times that are yet to come. This is called revelation or vision. If they are corporeal images, man apprehends them in his imagination. This indeed an angel achieves in man through the power of God. If it is some comprehensible truth or some spiritual likeness whereby God manifests Himself in all His profundity, then man apprehends it in his understanding, and he is able to reproduce it in words in so far as man has words for it. Sometimes man can be drawn above himself and above the spirit, but not in every respect outside himself, into an incomprehensible richness which he can never again find words for, or show as he heard and saw it: for in this single action and this single vision, to hear and to see are one and the same. And no-one can achieve this in man except God alone, without means and without the co-operation of any creature. This is called rapture, which is as much as to say carried off by force or overpowered.

Sometimes God gives to such men a brief glimpse in the spirit like the lightning of heaven. So there comes a brief glimpse of a peculiar clarity, and it shines out of a single bareness, and so in the twinkling of an eye the spirit is exalted above itself, and then at once the light is gone, and man comes to himself. God Himself performs this, and it is most excellent, because often by it men are enlightened. Sometimes these men who live in the tempest of love have another manner: for sometimes in them there shines a single light, and this God performs through means. In this light their hearts lift up, together with their capacity for desire, towards the light. And in this meeting with the light, the delight and the satisfaction is so great that the heart cannot endure it, but with joy bursts out in one cry: and this is called jubilation, which is to say a joy that is not to be told in words. And if man with upright and open heart meets with the light, he cannot forbear, but must continue to cry aloud for as long as the exercise and the manner last. Such inward men are instructed in dreams by means of their guardian angels or of other angels, and at such times learn of many things needful to them. One also finds such men who have fancies or inward voices or thoughts, and who yet remain in their senses without; and they dream marvellous things, yet they know nothing of the tempest of love, because they are not single, and are not wounded by love. This may come by way of nature, or from the devil, or from a man's good angel. And one may esteem this as highly as it resembles Holy Scripture and the truth, and no more: if one wishes to hold it in higher esteem, one may very easily be deceived.

4. *The obstacles to this way*

Now I wish to show you the hindrances and the harm that come to men who live in the tempest. At this time, as you have heard, the sun runs into the house of Leo, and that is the most unhealthy time of all the year, even if it is beneficial: for now the dog-days begin, which bring many plagues with them. Then at that time the season becomes so unnaturally hot that in such a land herbs and trees wither and dry up, in its waters some of the fish pine and perish, and on earth some men languish and die. And this is not only on account of the sun, for it happens in all lands alike, and in all waters and to all men: but it happens at this season because of the unnaturalness and intemperance of the material means through which the sun takes effect. And so in just the same way, when a man enters into this impatient way of living, he comes into his dog-days. And the shining of the Divine rays burns so fiercely and so hotly from above, and the loving, wounded heart is so enkindled from within, when the heart of the affections and the impatience of desires is so much enkindled, that man falls into impatience and dissatisfaction, just as a woman who labours with child and cannot be well. If then man will gaze without ceasing into his own wounded heart and upon Him Whom he loves, his woe will be always increasing. This torment increases so long that man's bodily nature withers and dries up, just as does the tree in a hot country; and in the tempest of love he dies, and without passing through the fires of purgatory he goes to heaven. Though he dies well who dies for love, so long as the tree is able to bear good fruit one should not destroy it.

Sometimes God flows with great sweetness into the tempestuous heart, and then in the waves of this sweetness the heart swims as the fish swim in the water, and the deepest depths of the heart burn in the tempest and in charity for this swimming in God's gifts, and for the rich and impatient heat of the loving heart; and to remain long in this state destroys man's bodily nature. In this state of being all tempestuous men must languish, but not all of them die, if they know well how to govern themselves.

And now I wish to warn you of a thing of which great harm may come. Sometimes in this hot season there falls honey-dew, which is nothing but a false sweetness, which taints or even destroys the fruit; and it is apt to fall in the middle of the day, in bright sunshine, with great drops, and it is hard to distinguish from rain. So in just the same way such men may be deprived of their senses from without by means of a single light that comes from the devil; and they are caught and snared in this light, and at this moment complex images compounded of truth and falsehood are shown and suggested to them. And they see and hear this to their great satisfaction. And here sometimes the honey-drops of false sweetness fall, when man finds this most pleasing. And if a man holds such an experience in great esteem, it will often happen to him, and so easily he will become tainted. But if he persists in regarding as true things which do not resemble the truth, because they have been shown or said to him, he will fall into error, and the fruits of his virtues will be lost for ever. But those who pursue the path which has been shown to them, even if they are tempted by such a spirit and such a light, cannot be harmed by it.

5. *A similitude of the ant*

I wish to give a short similitude to those who live and fare in the tempest, so that they may valiantly and obediently persist in this manner of living, and attain to high virtue. There is a little beast called the ant. She is strong and wise and hard to kill. And she loves to live in the company of her fellows in a hot, dry land. And she works in the summer and gathers up food and corn against the winter; and she splits each grain in two, so that it cannot germinate and spoil, but so that the ants can benefit from it when there is no other food to be had. And each ant does not make a separate path, but they all follow the same path. And when the season comes that she has been willing to wait for, then she is able to fly. Thus these men ought to do: they should be strong in awaiting the coming of Christ, wise against the revelations and suggestions of the devil. They must not wish for death, but always for the honour of God and to win for themselves fresh virtue. They must live in the company of their heart and all their powers, and be obedient to the demands and the compulsion of Divine unity. They must live in a hot, dry land, which is in the violent tempest of love and in great impatience, and they must work in their lives' summer, and gather the fruits of virtue against eternity, and split them in two. The one portion is that they

must evermore desire the high and delectable unity: the other
is that they must restrain themselves by means of reason,
so far as they may, and await the time that God has ordained:
so the fruit of virtues is preserved to all eternity. And they
must not make separate paths or peculiar manners for themselves, but they must follow the path of love through all the
storms on the way that love leads them. And while man awaits
his time, and furnishes himself with all virtues, he is able to
contemplate, and to flee into God's secret refuge.

d. *The fourth manner: man's forsakenness* (*cap. xii*)

Now let us go on to speak of the fourth manner of the
coming of Christ, which exalts and perfects man in inward
exercise in the lowest part of his humanity. But because we
have compared each inward coming with the shining of the
sun and its power, according to the progress of the year, so
let us go on to speak of other actions of the sun, according
to the advancement of the seasons.

1. *The sun in Virgo*

When the sun begins to decline sharply from the highest
part of heaven, it runs into the house of the sign known as
Virgo, because the season then becomes unfruitful, as a virgin
is. It was at this season that the glorious Virgin Mary, the
mother of Christ, went up into heaven, filled with joys and
rich in all virtues. At this season the heat begins to decrease,
and the timely durable fruits such as corn and wine and fruit,
which we can long after benefit from and use, which have
awaited their due season, it is the custom now for men to
gather in against the long winter. And men are accustomed to
sow from the same corn, so that it may be multiplied to the
benefit of mankind. So at this season all the work of the sun
throughout all the year is completed and made perfect. In just
the same way, when Christ the glorious Sun has ascended to
the highest point in the human heart, as I taught you when I
spoke of the third manner, and He then begins to decline and

to conceal the shining of His Divine rays, and to forsake man, so then the heat and the impatience of love begin to decline.

2. How Christ conceals Himself

The first work and the new coming of Christ in this manner is that He thus hides Himself and withdraws the radiance of His light and His heat. Now to such a man Christ says spiritually: 'Go out in the manner which I now show to you.'

3. The effect

So man goes out, and finds himself poor, exiled, forsaken. All the storm and violence and impatience of love is now cooled, and after the hot summer comes an autumn, after all riches great poverty. So man begins to complain, lamenting his lot: whither has the heat of love departed, with inwardness, thankfulness, praise and satisfaction: inward consolation, inward joy and sensible savour, where are they hiding: the violent tempest of love and all the gifts that ever he felt, how is it that they are dead to him? So he is just like an unlearned man who has lost profit and labour. Here nature is many a time robbed of its profits by such losses. Sometimes these wretched persons are robbed of worldly goods, of friends and kinsmen, and forsaken by all creatures, and unrecognized and unheeded by all the holy souls, and all their lives and all their works are misinterpreted by other men. And they are despised and rejected by all those who are near them. And sometimes they fall into various plagues and sicknesses. And such men fall into temptations of the body, or of the soul, which is worst of all. Out of this poverty comes a dread lest one should fall, and doubt on this account. This is the furthest point to which man can go without despairing. Then such a man will eagerly seek out good men and make his lament to them and show his misery, and he will ask the help and the prayers of Holy Church and the saints and of all good men.

4. Our response

Here a man should observe with a humble heart that he of

himself has nothing but want: and in patience and in abandonment of himself he shall say the words which Job, that holy
man, spoke: 'God gave, God took away: as it was pleasing
to the Lord, so did it happen; blessed be the name of the Lord.' [1]
And he shall abandon himself in all things, and say and intend
in his heart: 'Lord, I will as gladly be poor in the lack of all
this of which I have been robbed, as I would be rich, Lord,
if Thou wilt have it so and it be to Thine honour. Lord, not
my will according to nature, but Thy will and my will according
to Thy Spirit, let that be done, Lord,[2] for I am Thine, and I
would as gladly be in hell as in heaven, if it may do Thee
honour. Lord, in all virtuous things do with me that it be to
Thine excelling.' And out of all his desolation a man shall make
an inward joy, and offer himself into the hands of God, and
rejoice that he may suffer to the glory of God. If he prospers
in this manner, he will never yet have tasted so great an
inward joy: for there is nothing so satisfactory to God's lover
as that he feel that he is his Beloved's own. And he has climbed
the path of virtue straight to this manner, even if he has not
had all the manners which have been already shown here, for
that is not necessary, if he has felt the depths of virtue in
himself, that is to say, humble obedience in his works, and
patient resignation in suffering. This manner consists of these
two, in everlasting certainty. At this season of the year the
sun in the heavens runs into the house of Libra, for then day
and night are equal to each other, and the sun gives light to
balance the darkness. So in the same way Christ stands in the
balance against the forsaken man. Whether He gives sweet or
sour, darkness or light, whatever He puts into the balance,
man gives equal weight. All things are of equal weight to Him,
except sin alone, which must at this time be driven out.

When these men who have passed out of tempest into calm
are in this way deprived of all comfort, and, as it seems to them,
are finished with the anguish of love and are forsaken by God
and all His creatures, it is then that they are well able to gather
in their harvest of every kind, for the corn and the wine are

now ready, ripe and timely, for they have stood long in the sun. Everything that the body is able to suffer, in whatever fashion that may be, one should gladly and freely offer up to God, without any gainsaying of the *ratio superior*. All the outward or the inward anguish which one ever felt in delectable exercise in the fire of love, one must now exercise so far as intellect and strength permit, with labour and with a good heart, and offer all this up to God: for it was never yet so precious to Him as now, nor was it ever so excellent and so rare. Man must gladly forgo and lack all the consolation that God ever gave, so that it be to His honour. This is the gathering-in of the corn and of every timely fruit, on which man shall live and in which he shall be rich with God. Thus are virtues made perfect, and mistrust is turned into an everlasting wine. All who know such men and are together with them will be improved and instructed by them and by their life and by their patience. And so the grain of their virtues is sown and multiplied, to the profit of all good men. This is the fourth manner which adorns and perfects man in inward exercise according to his physical powers and to the lowest part of himself; and if it be not so, he may never advance on the path of growth and perfection without turning aside. But because such men are sorely tried and proved and tempted by God and their own natures and all creatures, and are assailed, the virtue of self-abandonment is in them a perfection particularly great, for to abandon and deny one's own will for the compulsion of God's will is needful to all men who wish to be preserved.

5. *The obstacles to this way*

Because now this season of the year is equinoxial, the sun begins to decline and the season to grow cold. And therefore evil humours, which fill up the stomach and cause indispositions and various sicknesses, oppress men who are careless of their health: and these humours deprive them of the delight and savour of all good food, and bring some such men to death. Because of evil humours some men suffer physical degeneration, and they are afflicted with dropsy, through which they languish for long and sometimes die. From a superfluity of humours come grave distempers and fevers, through which many men languish and sometimes die. So in the same way all men who are of good will or who have ever savoured God, and who thereafter fall off and wander away from God and from the truth, they all languish, because they do not pursue a straight path, or they die to virtue, or they suffer eternal death from one of these sicknesses, and sometimes from all three. And particularly in this abandonment man has need of great fortitude, and of exercise in the manner in which I have already instructed you: and if he does so he will never be deceived. But the unwise man who governs himself ill falls easily into such sickness, because in him the season has grown cold.

This is why man's nature grows weary of virtues and good works, and longs for bodily ease and comfort, sometimes immoderately and more than there is need of. And such men would gladly accept consolation from God, if He would bring it to them without their effort and labour; and such men seek solace in His creatures, from which many a time great harm comes to them; and it seems to such men that they are sick and delicate and enfeebled, and that they have need of every earthly thing they can attain, or that they must have rest and comfort for their bodies. When a man thus imprudently inclines himself and is obedient to earthly things and bodily comfort, these are all evil humours which swell the stomach, that is the human heart, and take away from him the savour and the delight in all good food, that is in all virtues. When man thus falls into sickness and into frigidity, he is sometimes afflicted with dropsy. That is an inclination towards the visible possession of earthly things. The more these men obtain, the more they covet, because they suffer from dropsy. Their body, which is appetite and delight, becomes greatly distended, and their thirst is never appeased. But their face, which is conscience and judgment, becomes little and thin, because they oppose hindrances and obstacles to the influence of the grace of God. If their hearts are oppressed with the dropsy of the water of earthly possession, that is that they take delight and rest there, they cannot go forward in works of charity, because they are sick. Their spirits and their breath are too short: that is, they lack the grace of God and inward charity. And therefore they cannot void the water of earthly possession, but their hearts are beset with it, and often it happens that through this they languish in eternal death. But those whom the water of earthly things oppresses far beneath the heart, so they have power over their possessions and can become free of them when there is need, even though they may languish for long in inordinate inclination, they may well recover even so.

These men who are filled with evil humours, that is to say who live in inordinate inclination towards bodily savour and towards the consolations, separating them from God, of His creatures, fall sometimes into four kinds of fever.

The first fever is called quotidian, which is diversity of heart. For these men wish to know about everything and give their opinion on everything and dispute and correct everything: and very often they forget about themselves. They bear many men's sorrows: many a time they must listen to what displeases them: one can perturb them with trifles: their sufferings are of many kinds, now for this, now for that, now here, now there, like to the wind. This is a quotidian fever, because through it they are oppressed and preoccupied and distraught from morning till evening, and sometimes in the night, sleeping and waking. Even though this state of things may be consonant with the grace of God and without deadly sin, it still hinders inwardness and interior exercise and man's savour of God and of the virtues, and this is an everlasting harm.

The second fever, the tertian fever which comes every other day, is the name I give to instability. Though it is slower in developing, it is often more grievous. This fever is of a double nature: one nature comes from inordinate heat, the other from cold. Those men whose nature is compounded of intemperate heat have sometimes a robust physique. But if they are touched by God, or have been touched, and thereafter are abandoned by Him, they then often fall into instability. Today they will choose one manner of living, tomorrow another, and so they will go on; at one time they wish to keep silence, at another they wish to speak; now they wish to join this religious order, now that; today they wish to give away all their goods for God's sake, tomorrow they wish to keep them; today they wish to wander abroad, and tomorrow to shut themselves up in a cloister; today they desire to go frequently to Holy Communion, and in a short time they have little regard for it; for a while all their wish is to read much, and then after a short period to keep silence. This is nothing but newfangledness and instability, which hinders and prevents man from understanding inward truth, and deprives him of the foundation and the exercise of all inwardness. Now understand whence comes this instability in good men. If a man fixes upon virtue and outward forms as the objects of his intention and his labours, more than upon God and unity with God, then even if he remain in God's grace, because in virtue it is God Whom he intends, his life is still unstable, because he does not feel himself to be resting in God above all virtues. And therefore he possesses that of which he knows nothing. For Him Whom he searches for in virtues and in various outward forms he possesses within himself, above intention and above virtue and above all forms. Therefore if a man is to conquer this instability, he must learn to rest, above all virtue, in God and in His high unity.

The other kind of instability, which comes from cold, afflicts all those men who intend God and who set up something as equal to Him, which they inordinately seek and intend. This kind of fever comes from cold because there is little heat of charity where things alien to God strive and contend with Him in man's works of virtue. Such people are unstable of heart, because in all things which they do, human nature seeks secretly to attain its own ends, very often without their knowledge, because they do not know themselves as they should. These men will choose this way of life and renounce that way of life today, and tomorrow something different. Today they wish to go to one man for absolution, and for counsel about all their lives, tomorrow they will choose someone else. They wish to ask for counsel in every matter: seldom do they want to follow anyone's counsel. If anyone misprizes or ridicules them in anything, they are very eager to excuse and gloze it. They have many fine words, but there is little in them. Always they are eager to have the credit for virtues, but only to perform little deeds. They crave to have their virtues made known, and that is why they are empty and have no savour of God. They want to teach other men, and never to be taught or rebuked. It is their natural inclination towards themselves and their hidden arrogance which makes these men unstable. These people are walking round the edge of hell: let them take another false step and they will fall in.

Out of this kind of instability there comes in some men at times the quartan fever, which is in man an alienation from God and from himself, and from truth and all virtue. And so man falls into a dazed condition, in which he does not know where he is afflicted or what he ought to do. This sickness is more grievous than any of the others. And out of this alienation man sometimes falls into that kind of fever which is called the double quartan, which is indifference. Then is the quartan fever of doubled strength, and once it is come a man may never be well again, for he becomes reckless and indifferent of everything which is necessary to his eternal life. Thus he may fall into sin as does a man who knows nothing of God. If this can happen to those who govern themselves ill when they are so forsaken, how much care should they have who know nothing of God nor of the interior life, nor of that inward savour which good men have in their exercises.

e. *An example: how in Christ we shall find the perfection of these four manners (cap. xiii)*

We must go in the light, so that we do not stray, and we must observe Christ, Who has taught us these four manners of living and has gone before to show us the way, Christ the bright Sun, Who rose into the heaven of the high Trinity, and Whose dawn was His glorious mother the Virgin Mary, who was and is a dawn and a beginning of that day of all graces in which we shall everlastingly rejoice. Now observe: Christ had and indeed still has the first manner: for He was single and united. In Him were and are assembled and united all the virtues which existed or ever shall exist, and, still more, all the creatures who performed or shall perform these virtues. Thus He was the only Son of the Father, and united with human nature. And He was inward, for He brought upon earth that fire which has enkindled all saints and all good men, and He bore a sensible love and faith towards His Father and towards all those who shall everlastingly enjoy Him. And His devotion and His loving and enduring heart yearned and burned before His Father all His lifetime for the need of all mankind; and all His works, exterior and interior, and all His words were the thanks and the praise and the honour of His Father. This is the first manner.

Christ that dear Sun appeared and shone more brightly and with greater heat, because in Him there was and is the perfection of all graces and all gifts. And therefore Christ's heart and His manner and His conversation and His service flowed out in mercifulness and in meekness and in humility and in mildness. And He was so gracious and so lovable that His conversation and His being drew all men after Him who were of good natures. He was the unsmirched lily, and the wild flower of the fields,[1] whence all good men bring away the honey of everlasting sweetness and everlasting consolation. Christ in His humanity thanked and praised His eternal Father for all the gifts that were ever given to His humanity, Him Who is the only Father of all bounties and all gifts. And in the highest powers of His soul He rested above all gifts in the high unity of God, whence all gifts flow out. And thus Christ had the second manner.

Christ the glorious Sun appeared and shone yet higher and

[1] Cf. Song of Solomon ii 1-2.

with greater light and heat; for all the days of His life, His physical and His sensual powers, His heart and mind were required and demanded of Him by His Father, to the greater glory and blessing of that Father Whom Christ tasted according to His physical powers, and towards Whom He was in His affections inclined, naturally and supernaturally. Nevertheless He was willing to await in this exile the time which the Father in eternity had foreseen and foreordained. And thus He had the third manner.

When the fitting time came, when Christ wished to lead and to gather into the everlasting kingdom all the fruits of the virtues which ever had been performed or shall be performed, then the eternal Sun began to decline. For Christ abased Himself, and gave His mortal life into the hands of His enemies, and when He was in such straits He was disavowed and forsaken by His friends. And His humanity was deprived of all consolation from without and from within, and upon it was laden misery and torment and shame, and the load and burden and ransom of all sins, which He in righteousness must pay; and this He bore in humble patience. And in this desolation He performed the valiant deed of love, and through it He gained and obtained for us our eternal inheritance. Thus was He adorned in the lowest part of His most excellent humanity, for it was in this humanity that for our sins He suffered this labour. And therefore He is called the preserver of the world, and is transfigured and glorified and exalted and set at the right hand of His Father, and reigns in power. And every creature bows the knee, in heaven and earth and hell, before His great name, world without end.

1. *The first coming makes ready for the second*

When a man lives in moral virtues in due obedience according to God's commandments, and furthermore in justness and due proportion exercises himself in interior virtues, according to the manner and the passion of the Holy Spirit, as the Spirit draws him and speaks within him, and when in this he seeks for nothing for himself, neither in time nor in eternity, and is able to balance and to bear darkness and heaviness and misery of every kind in righteous patience, and thanks God for it all and offers it up to Him in patient resignation, then he has received the first coming of Christ according to the manner of inward exercise. And in his interior life he has gone out, and is adorned in himself with precious virtues and with graces, with a heart that is quickened, and with living, sensible unity. When man in the lowest part of his nature is well purged and established and withdrawn, he may then be inwardly illumined, when it seems timely to God and He commands it. And it may indeed well happen that he is illumined at the beginning of his conversion, in order that he may wholly offer himself to the will of God and deny every claim of his own being: upon that all things depend. But afterwards he must follow the way and the manner which have been shown here previously, both in his exterior and his interior life, and that ought to be easier for him than for another man who makes his way up from below, for he was given more light than was the other man.

B. The second coming, in our highest powers, compared to a fount with three streams (*cap. xiv*)

Now let us go on to speak of the second manner of the coming of Christ in inward exercise, through which man is adorned and illumined and enriched, according to the three highest powers of the soul. Let us liken this coming to a living fount of water with three streams. This fount from which these streams flow forth is the abundance of God's grace in the unity of our spirit. Therein grace contains itself, in essence, as the spirit remains within itself, as does an abundant well; and in our works as we flow out with streams in every power of the soul according to its needs. These streams are God's special influences or inward workings in the highest powers of the soul, where God works by means of grace in many manners.

a. *The first stream: the gathering of our recollection (cap. xv)*

1. *The coming*

The first stream of God's grace which He causes to flow in this coming is a pure singleness which illumines the whole spirit without any difference. This stream has its source in the fount in the unity of the spirit, and it flows straight down and waters all the powers of the soul, the highest as well as the lowest, and raises the soul above all multiplicity that comes of preoccupation, and makes a singleness in man, and shows and gives to him an inward bond in the unity of his spirit. In this way, as concerns the power of the memory, man is exalted, and is set free from all disturbance from without, and from instability. Now Christ demands in this light that man should go out in the manner of the light and of His coming.

2. *Our response*

So man goes out, and observes and finds himself to be made apt and stable, by means of this single light that is shone within him, and to be transfused and preserved in the unity of his spirit or of his thoughts. Here man is exalted and set in a new manner of life, and turns within himself, and trains his memory to be bare, above all disturbance of images of the senses, and above multiplicity. Here man possesses naturally and supernaturally the unity of his spirit, as it were his own dwelling, and is made heir in perpetuity of himself. Thus he has naturally and supernaturally an inclination towards this same unity, and through the gift of God and through his own single intention this same unity shall have an eternal loving inclination towards that exalted unity where the Father and the Son in the bond of the Holy Spirit are united with all the saints. And thus is man filled full of this first river, that demands unity of him.

b. *The second stream: the illumining of our understanding (cap. xvi)*

1. *The coming*

Out of a fullness of grace, in this unity of the spirit, through inward love and a loving inclination and godly truth there springs the second river, which is a spiritual clarity which waters and illumines the comprehension, bringing with it a manifold perception. For the light shows and gives in the truth perception of all virtues. Yet to achieve this is not altogether in our power. For even though we always have this light within our souls, it is God who makes it to keep silence and to speak, God who can reveal it and conceal it, give it and take it away in what time and place He chooses; for the light is His. And therefore He works in this light as He pleases, and where He pleases, and in whom He pleases, and to what end He pleases. Such men have no need of any revelation, nor of being moved in manners unattainable by the senses, for their life and their dwelling and their conversation and their being is in the spirit, above the senses and above sensuality; and there God shows to them what He pleases which is needful to them or to other men. Yet, if it pleased Him, God could deprive such men of their outward senses, and from within show to them in many manners strange images and things which are yet to come. And now it is the will of Christ that such a man should go forth and fare in this light, according to the manner of the light.

2. *Our response*

Thus then this enlightened man shall go forth, and observe his own state and his life, from within and from without, and whether he bears a perfect image of Christ, in His humanity and in His Divinity. For we are made in the image and in the likeness of God. And he shall cast up his enlightened eyes, the truth being made comprehensible to him and his reason being illumined, and he shall observe and contemplate, so far as God's creatures may, His exalted nature and the inexhaustible qualities that are in Him. For to a nature that is inexhaustible belong inexhaustible virtues and deeds.

In the exalted nature of the Divinity he shall observe and contemplate that it is all simplicity and unity, heights unattainable and depths unfathomable; incomprehensible depth and everlasting length; a dark silence and a vast desert; the everlasting rest of all the saints, and the enjoyment of God and of His saints in all eternity. And still man can see many a wonder in the boundless sea of the Divinity. Even though, because of the crudeness of our senses, we make sensual images of that which we show forth, yet still in truth it is observed within and seen to be riches immeasurable and without manner. But because man must communicate it, so he attributes to it many kinds of images and manners, so that it may be illumined to the reason of him who shows and proclaims it. This enlightened man shall also mark and observe what is the attribute of the Father in the Godhead, how He is almighty strength and power, creator, supporter, mover, beginning and end, and the prime cause of all His creatures. The river of grace makes this manifest in clarity to the enlightened reason. And the river shows too the attributes of the everlasting Word: unfathomable wisdom and truth; the pattern and the way of life for all creatures; the everlasting rule that is immutable; the contemplation and the scrutiny of all things, from which nothing is hidden; the illumination and the enlightenment of all saints in heaven and in earth according to their merit. Since now this river of clarity gives many kinds of discernment, it also shows to the enlightened reason what are the attributes of the Holy Spirit: incomprehensible charity and mildness; pity and grace; endless fidelity and benevolence; an outflowing richness incomprehensibly great, and a limitless goodness, flowing in blessedness through all heavenly spirits; a fiery flame that consumes all things in unity, a fountain flowing rich in savour according to the yearning of every man; the preparation and the leading-in of all saints to their eternal blessedness; the bond and the uniting of the Father and of the Son and of all saints in the unity which they enjoy.

All this is seen and contemplated, singly and without any division, in a simple nature of the Divinity. And yet these attributes, as we see them, are seen according to our powers of perception, and so by each man differently: for according as each of us perceives them, there is great difference in power and liberality, mercy and truth. Yet all are united and indivisible in the exalted nature of the Divinity. But the relationships which are caused by the attributes of the Persons consist in an eternal difference; for difference is born of the Father. For His Son is everlastingly born of the Father, Who Himself is not begotten. And the Son is begotten, Who Himself may not beget. Thus has the Father everlastingly and in eternity a Son, and the Son a Father; and these are the relations of the Father to the Son, and of the Son to the Father. And the Father and the Son breathe one Spirit, Who is the will and the delight of Them both. And this Spirit begets not nor is begotten, but He, flowing out from both of Them, may eternally be breathed. And these three Persons are one God and one Spirit. And all the attributes, with all the works which flow out from them, are common to all the Persons, for they operate through the powers of a single nature.

The incomprehensible riches and exaltation and the mildness and liberality with which the Divine nature makes itself common: all this makes man to be astonished. And particularly and above all things man is astonished to see how God makes Himself common, and the liberality of it: for he perceives that in this incomprehensible nature of God consists the enjoyment of Him which He shares with all the saints. And he perceives in the Divine Persons a common flowing-out and working, in grace and in glory, in nature and above nature, in all states and in all times, in saints and in men, in heaven and in earth, in all creatures, rational or irrational or inanimate, according to each one's worth and need and capacity to receive. And he sees heaven and earth created, sun and moon and the four elements, together with all creatures and the courses of heaven, all of them indifferently created. For God is indifferent in the giving of all His gifts. The angels are indifferent, and the soul is indifferent in all powers and in all bodies and in all members. And the soul is everywhere, among all the members, for man cannot divide it as it might seem to the reason. For the superior and inferior powers, the spirit and the soul are different according to reason, yet in nature all is one. Thus God is everywhere, in each and every creature, and yet is He common to them all; for all things exist through Him, and in Him and on Him depend heaven and earth and all nature.[1] Thus when man observes the marvellous richness and the exaltedness of the Divine natures, and all the multiplicity of gifts which God gives and proffers to His creatures, so within him there grows an astonishment at this multiplicity and richness and exaltedness and at the limitless love that He has for His creatures. And from this there springs a special inward rejoicing of the spirit, and a great confidence in God. And this inward rejoicing surrounds and transfuses all the powers of the soul and all the unity of the spirit.

c. *The third stream: the enkindling of the will (cap. xvii)*

Out of this joy and fullness of grace, and out of a Divine love, there springs and flows in this same unity of the spirit the third stream. This stream enkindles the will as if it flowed fire, and devours and consumes all things in unity, and waters and transfuses all the powers of the soul with rich gifts and with rare excellence, and without effort it makes in the will a subtle spiritual love. Now Christ through this burning river says inwardly in the spirit: 'Go out in exercises, according to the manner of these gifts and of this coming.'

1. *The coming*

Through the first stream, which is a single light, the recollection is exalted above influences of the senses, and settled and made steadfast in a unity of the spirit. Through the second stream, which is a clarity suddenly sent, the understanding and reason are enlightened to recognize virtues of every kind, and to distinguish the uses and the secrets of the Scriptures. Through the third stream, which is a heat breathed into us, the highest part of the will is enkindled in a secret love and endowed with great riches. Thus is this man become a spiritually enlightened man. For the grace of God is contained,

[1] Cf. Romans xi 36.

as if it were a well of water, in unity of the spirit. And the streams make in the faculties of man a flowing-out with all virtues. And the well of grace thus demands evermore a flowing back again into that same depth from which the flowing-out came forth.

2. *Our response*

Now man must remain steadfast, secure in the bond of love and dwelling in the unity of his spirit: and he must go out with an enlightened reason and with a charity that overflows towards heaven and earth, and he must observe all things with a lucid discretion, and he must give all things out of his righteous mercifulness and his Divine riches. These enlightened men are incited and disposed to go out in four manners. The first manner is towards God and towards all the saints. The second manner is towards sinners and all men who have gone astray. The third going out is into purgatory. And the fourth is towards himself and towards all good men.

Now understand that a man must go out and observe God in His glory with all the saints; and he shall contemplate the riches and the mercy with which God flows, with glories and with Himself and with incomprehensible delights, in all His saints, according to the desire of every spirit. And how they flow back again with themselves and with all that they have received and with all of which they are capable, into that same rich unity whence all delight proceeds. This flowing of God demands evermore a flowing back again; for God is a sea, ebbing and flowing, ceaselessly flowing into each one of His elect, according to the needs and worth of each. And in His ebbing He draws back again all men to whom He has given in heaven and in earth, with all that they have and all of which they are capable. And from such men He demands more than they can achieve. For He manifests Himself to them so rich and so merciful and so immeasurably good, and in this manifestation He demands of them love and honour according to His worth. For God wishes to be loved by us in accordance with His excellence, and in this work all spirits fail; and so

9   127

love is without manner and without fashion. For our spirits do not know how to add yet more to the love that they already bear, for each spirit's capacity for love is finite. And therefore the work of love is constantly begun afresh, so that God may be loved as He demands and as they desire. And therefore all spirits evermore are gathered together and form one burning flame in love, so that they may bring to perfection the work of loving God according to His excellence. To the reason it is plain that this work is impossible for God's creatures. But love will always perfect love, or else in its failing melt and burn away to nothing. Yet God remains unloved, according to His worth, by all His creatures. And to men of enlightened reason this is a great delight and satisfaction, that their God and their Love is so exalted and so rich that He is exalted above all created powers, and that He is not loved by anyone save by Himself according to His worth. The man made thus rich and enlightened gives out of the riches of his God to all the choirs of angels and to all the blessed spirits, and to each one separately according to his worth, and out of the mercifulness in which he himself is established, a mercifulness enlightened and transfused with great marvels. He wanders among all the choirs and all those in blessedness and all created things, and he observes how God dwells in each according to his excellence. This enlightened man wanders swiftly abroad in the spirit, rich and overflowing in charity, and he goes among all the heavenly host, making all the cohorts of heaven to be rich and to overflow in fresh glories; and all this proceeds from the rich and overflowing Trinity and Unity of the Divine nature. This is the first going-out towards God and towards His saints.

This man shall sometimes descend to sinners with great compassion and with tender pity, and draw them up towards God with his inward devotions and with much prayer; and admonish them concerning God, of all the goodness that He is and that He does and that He has done to us and has promised, just as though they had forgotten this. For He will be adored; and charity will have all that it desires. Though

charity will not be stubborn nor obstinate, yet it demands all
the great riches and the mercifulness of God; for God loves
without measure. And in this the lover finds his most lasting
satisfaction. Because the love that this man now bears is an
indifferent love, he prays and longs that God should let His
love and His compassion flow out to heathens and to Jews and
to all unbelievers, so that He be loved and acknowledged in
the kingdom of heaven, and so that our glory and joy and
peace be increased in every quarter of the earth. This is the
second going out to sinners.

Sometimes man must behold his friends in purgatory, and
mark their misery and their longing and their cruel torment.
Then must he implore and call upon the grace and the mercy
and the mildness of God, and show to Him their good will and
their great misery and their desire for the great riches of God.
And he must call to God's recollection that they died in His
love, and that all their confidence is in His Passion and His
grace. Now understand, sometimes it may happen that this
enlightened man may be impelled particularly by the Spirit
of God to pray for some one thing, for a sinner or for a soul
or for some spiritual grace, so that he sees indeed and proves
that this comes by the influence of the Holy Ghost, and is not
of obstinacy or wilfulness or human nature. So sometimes man
is so enrapt and so inspired in his prayer that he receives a
spiritual answer that his prayer has been heard, and at this
same sign the passion of the spirit and the prayer cease.

Now man must come to himself and to all men who are of
good will, and he must savour and observe how they are
drawn together and of one mind in their love, and he must
desire and pray of God that He let flow all His customary gifts,
so that these men remain steadfast in His love and in His
eternal honour. This enlightened man shall instruct and teach
all men, admonish and serve them, faithfully and in moderation; for his love is for all men. And therefore he is inter-
mediary between God and all men. And with integrity he shall
turn inward into himself, together with all the saints and all
good men, and in peace possess the unity of his spirit, and

furthermore the exalted unity of God wherein all spirits rest. This is a true spiritual life, for all manners and all virtues, internal and external, and the highest powers of the soul are through it supernaturally adorned, as is right and due.

3. *A deviation from this way*

One finds certain men who are indeed subtle in their speech and apt to show forth high matters, and yet they have no savour of this enlightened way, nor of this common love in mercifulness. So that these men may be able to instruct themselves, and also be known to other men, I wish to show you what they are, under three headings. Under the first heading they shall be able to recognize themselves. Under the other two each man who has understanding shall be able to recognize them. First: whereas an enlightened man is in his nature simple and steadfast and inconspicuous, by means of Divine enlightenment, they are diverse and infirm and full of care and remarkable in men's eyes, nor do they savour any inward unity nor any tranquillity free from mental images. And in this they shall be able to recognize themselves. The second point is that whereas the enlightened man has a wisdom sent down to him from God, wherein he knows and discerns the truth without labour, these men have accesses of subtility, and on these they build mental images, and they compose and observe with curious skill. But such a man is not plentiful nor bounteous in bringing forth teaching, and his teaching is diverse and of strange matters and subtle, leading astray men who are truly inward, and hindering them and disquieting them. For his teaching does not point the way and lead to unity, but it instructs men to be skilled in the contemplation of diversity. Such people are obstinate in the defence of their teaching and mode of thought, even though some other mode might be as good as theirs. And they are lukewarm and careless of all virtues. They are full of spiritual pride in all their lives. This is the second point. The third point is that the enlightened, loving man flows out to all men in charity in heaven and on earth, as you have heard, whereas

in all things these men go their own way. It seems to them
that they are the wisest and the best of all men. They wish men
to hold them and their teaching in great esteem. Everything
which they do not teach and counsel they deem to be error,
and those who do not follow their manner and pay heed to
them they condemn. They are great in their demands and they
pay small heed to their light defaults. Such men are not just or
humble or mild, they are not serviceable to the poor or
inwardly devout or zealous, nor are they sensible of the Divine
love, nor are they true and patient in seeking knowledge of
God or of themselves. This is the third point. Mark these
things, and make them known, and look for them in yourselves
and in all men in whom you may recognize them. And do not
condemn such things in any man, unless they are made manifest
by his deeds: for to do otherwise would hinder your heart
from recognizing the Divine truth.

4. *Christ as our example*

So that we may possess this common way of life, and desire
it above all other ways of which we have spoken, because
it is the highest, so let us take Christ as our exemplar, Who was
and is and shall be to all eternity the shepherd of us all. For
He was sent upon earth for all men, to the profit of them who
will turn to Him. Yet does He Himself say that He was not
sent to others than the sheep who are lost out of the House
of Israel.[1] These are not only the Jews, but all who shall
eternally contemplate God, they and no-one else. For the Jews
despised the Gospel, and the heathen came and received it,
and thus was all Israel preserved, which is all the eternally
chosen.

Now observe how Christ in His true love gave Himself in
common to all men. His most fervent and exalted prayer
flowed out to His Father, and in common to all those who wish
to be preserved. Christ was common to all men in His love,
His teaching, His admonition; in consolation with meekness;
in giving with mildness; in forgiving with mercifulness and

[1] St. Matthew x 5.

131

pity. His soul and His body, His life and His death and His mission, all were and are common to all men. His sacraments and His gifts are common. Christ never received food nor any other necessity of the body, but it was to the common profit of those who shall be saved until the Day of Judgment. Christ had neither property nor possession, but all was in common: body and soul, mother and disciples, cloak and coat. He ate and He drank for our sake; He lived and He died for our sake. His torment and His suffering and His misery were His, and His alone, but the profit and the benefit that came from them is common to all, and the glory He achieved shall be common to all eternally.

Now Christ has left here upon earth His treasures and His revenues, which are the seven sacraments, and the worldly possessions of Holy Church, which He earned with His death, and which should be common to all. And His servants who live on these possessions, they too should be common to all men. All those who live upon alms and are in religion, they should be common, at least in their prayers, those such as men and women of religion, and those who live in cloisters and enclosures. In the beginnings of Holy Church and of our Faith, popes, bishops and priests were common, for they converted the people, and built Holy Church and our belief, and they set their seal on their work with their death and with their blood. These were simple and single-minded men, and they enjoyed a lasting peace in their unity of the spirit; and they were enlightened with Divine truth, and they were rich and overflowing in love and charity towards God and all men. But now everything is the contrary. For those men who now possess the heritage and the revenues, which were given to those others out of love and for the sake of their sanctity, are men of unstable life, insecure and distracted; for they have turned themselves to the world, and have no proper care for the things and the causes that they should be concerned with. Therefore they pray with their lips, but their hearts have no savour of the prayer and what it signifies,[1] which is the secret

[1] Cf. St. Matthew xv 8.

miracle concealed within the Scriptures and in the sacraments and in their office; of all this they have no perception. And therefore are they so dull and obtuse and unenlightened by Divine truth. And some of them seek to eat and drink well, and inordinately they covet ease of the body, and would to God that they were even clean in their lives. As long as they live thus, they shall never be enlightened. And just as much as those of old times were mild and overflowing in charity, and retained nothing for themselves, so now these men are many of them grasping and avaricious, nor will they forgo anything. This is all completely contrary and unlike to the saints and to the common way of life of which we have spoken. I speak of affairs as they generally are: let each man examine himself, and instruct and reprimand himself if he have need of it. And should he have no need of it, let him have joy and rest and peace in his good conscience, and let him serve and love God, and be of profit to himself and to all men in God's honour. Because I wish particularly to extol and praise this common way of life, so I have found yet another particular jewel which Christ bequeathed to all good men in common in Holy Church. At supper at the high feast of the Passover, when Christ wished to pass from this exile to His Father, when He had eaten the paschal lamb with His disciples, and all the old law was fulfilled, at the end of the meal and of the feast, He wished to serve them with a special dish, for He had long desired to keep this feast with them; and doing this, He wished to end the old law and to begin the new. And He took bread in His honourable and venerable hands, and consecrated His holy body and thereafter His holy blood, and gave them in common to His disciples, and bequeathed them in common to all good men to their everlasting profit.[1] This gift and this dish gladdens and adorns our every high feast and every banquet, in heaven and in earth. In this gift, God gives Christ to us in three manners. He gives to us His flesh and His blood and His bodily life, glorified, full of joys and sweetnesses. And

---

[1] These two sentences are in part a paraphrase of the prayer of consecration from the Canon of the Mass.

He gives to us His spirit, with the highest powers, full of glories and gifts, truths and righteousness. And He gives to us His personality, with Divine clarity, which exalts His spirit and all enlightened spirits into the exalted and enjoyable unity.

Now Christ would have us commemorate Him as often as we consecrate, offer and receive His body. Now observe how we should commemorate Him. We should observe and behold how Christ abases Himself to us, in loving affection and great desire and in delight of His whole being, and with an outflowing of His heart into our bodily natures. For He gives to us that which He took upon Himself of our humanity, that is His flesh and blood and bodily nature. We should also observe and behold how this precious body was tormented and scarred and wounded by love and joy for our sake. With this are we adorned and fed, in the lowest part of our humanity, with Christ's glorious humanity. In this exalted gift of the sacrament He gives us also His spirit full of glories, of rich gifts and virtues and ineffable miracles of charities and excellences. And with this we are feasted and adorned and illumined in the unity of our spirit and in our highest powers, through the indwelling of Christ with all His riches. And more He gives to us in the sacrament of the altar: His exalted personality, in incomprehensible clarity. And through this we are united and taken up to the Father. And the Father receives His elected Son together with his begotten Son. And thus we come into our inheritance of the Divinity in everlasting blessedness.

When man has meditated and contemplated this as is due, then he shall meet Christ in all the manners in which Christ comes to him. He shall raise himself up to receive Christ with his heart, with his desires, with his sensible love, with all his powers and with the delight of his desire. And thus shall Christ receive him. And this delight may never be too great, for our nature takes upon it the nature of delight, which is the nature of Christ's humanity, glorified, full of joys and honours. And it is for this reason that I would have man, in this receiving, to melt and flow away in desire, in joy and in bliss. For he receives and is united with Him Who is the fairest, the most gracious, the most lovable, above all the sons of men. In this delectable impelling and in this delight, oftentimes riches are conferred upon man, and many a secret and hidden marvel is made manifest and revealed to him out of the great riches of God. When man in this receiving meditates upon the torment and the suffering of this precious body of Christ Whom he receives, he attains at times to such a loving devotion and such a sensible compassion that he longs to be nailed with Christ to the cross, and he longs to shed his heart's blood in Christ's honour. And he flees for refuge into the wounds and riven heart of Christ his preserver. In this exercise of devotion, often it is granted to man that many things are made known and that great gifts are made to him. This sensible love that has compassion, and this powerful imagining that fervently ponders the wounds of Christ, may be so great that it shall seem to man that he has felt the wounds and the torments of Christ in his heart and in all his limbs. And should any man truly receive in any manner the stigmata of the wounds of Our Lord, it should be this man. And in this way we gratify Christ in the lowest part of His humanity. We should also dwell in the unity of our spirit, and flow out with an ample charity in heaven and in earth, with a lucid discretion. And in this way we bear the likeness of Christ in spirit, and so gratify Him. We should also, by means of Christ's personality, with a single intention and with delectable love, pass beyond ourselves and beyond the humanity of Christ, and have rest in our heritage, which is the Divine nature in eternity. Christ is ever desirous to grant this to us in the spirit, as often as we exercise ourselves in this way and make a place ready for Him within us. And He wills that we should receive Him, sacramentally and spiritually, as often as it is fitting and proper or advisable. Even though man may not have all these feelings and all these desires, yet if he intend the praise and honour of God, and his own advancement and blessedness, he may freely approach the table of Our Lord, so long as his conscience is free from deadly sin.

C. The Third Coming: the Touching in the Unity of the Spirit

a. *How God from out of His unity moves the soul in its unity (cap. xviii)*

1. The exalted and supernatural unity of the Divine nature, where the Father and the Son possess Their nature in the unity of the Holy Ghost, above all the comprehension and understanding of which we are capable, in the naked being of our spirit; in this exalted stillness God exceeds every thought of His creatures. This exalted unity of the Divine nature is a living, fertile unity. For out of this same unity the Everlasting Word is evermore born of the Father, and through this birth the Father acknowledges the Son and in the Son all things. And the Son acknowledges the Father and in the Father all things, for They are one single nature. And out of this mutual contemplation of the Father and the Son in Their eternal illumination, there flows an eternal satisfaction, an unfathomable love, and that is the Holy Spirit. And through the Holy Spirit and the everlasting wisdom, God inclines Himself in discretion towards each one of His creatures, and gives to each one and enkindles him in love according to his excellence and according to the state in which he is and is chosen through his virtues and the eternal providence of God. And through this are all good spirits moved, in heaven and in earth, in virtues and in righteousness. Now pay heed, for I wish to show you a similitude concerning this.

2. *A similitude of how God naturally and supernaturally possesses and moves the soul*

God has created the highest heaven to be a pure and single clarity, enfolding and surrounding all the heavens and all things, animate and inanimate, which God ever created. For this is an exterior dwelling place and a kingdom of God and of His saints, filled full of glories and of eternal joy. Now because this heaven is an everlasting and unmingled clarity, there is therefore neither time there nor place, nor any motion nor mutation of any sort, for it is established and immutable above all things. The lowest sphere of this empyrean heaven is called the *primum mobile*. Out of this there springs through the power of God all motion. Out of this motion the firmament and all the planets have their revolution, and through it all creatures live and grow, each one according to its nature.

Now understand that in just the same way the existence of the soul is a spiritual kingdom of God, filled full of Divine clarity, exceeding all our powers, even though this may not be in any single manner; but concerning this I will at this time not speak. Observe how from this existence of the soul in which God reigns, the unity of our spirit is maintained, just as in the case of the *primum mobile*; for in this unity the spirit is moved from above in the power of God, naturally and supernaturally. For of ourselves we have nothing natural or supernatural. And this motion of God, as it is supernatural, is then the first and prime cause of all virtue. And in the motion of God are given to such enlightened men the seven gifts of the Holy Ghost, just as in the case of the seven planets, which enlighten and make fruitful all mortal existence. This is the way in which God possesses the essential unity of our spirit as His kingdom, and in which He works and flows out with gifts into all our powers and into our souls, as they are capable of unity with Him.

b. *How man must be adorned, if he is to receive the most fervent spiritual exercise (cap. xix)*

Now observe with care how we after the created light of reason must pursue and possess the most fervent exercise of our spirit. The man who in his exterior life is well adorned with moral virtues, and in his excellence has ascended with fervent exercise and in godly peace, possesses a unity of his spirit, enlightened with supernatural wisdom, flowing out in merciful charity in heaven and earth, and rising up and flowing back again, bringing with it honours and worth, into the same depths and into the high unity of God whence all flowing forth proceeds: for every creature, as he is more and more enriched by God, has in this measure a love rising higher and higher, and is fervently impelled back to the source of love. For God and all His gifts impel us to return into Him, and we through charity and virtue and our likeness to God desire to be in Him.

c. The Divine touching: of the third coming of Christ, which perfects us in the interior exercise (cap. xx)

Through the loving inclination of God, and through His interior working in the fervour of our spirit, and through our burning love and the great effort which we make with all our powers to enter into that same unity in which God dwells, there springs the third coming of Christ in inward exercises. And this is an inward touching by Christ in His Divine clarity upon the innermost part of our spirit. The second coming of which we have spoken we likened to a living source with three streams. But let us liken this coming to the springs that feed the sources, for there is no river without its source, nor is there source without its living springs. And so, just in the same way, the grace of God flows in rivers into the highest powers of the soul, and impels and enkindles men in all virtues. And grace gathers in the unity of our spirit as a source, and flows into that same unity whence it springs, just as a living, flowing spring from the living depths of the riches of God, where love and grace may nevermore run dry. And this is the touching which I mean. And the creature suffers and endures this touching, for here there is a uniting of the highest powers in the unity of the spirit, above the multiplicity of all virtues. And in this there is no person operative but God alone, out of His free liberality, Who is the sole cause of all our virtue and all our blessedness. In the unity of the spirit, where this spring flows, man is above working and above reason, but he is not without reason; for the enlightened reason, and in particular the power of the soul to love, feels this touching, yet reason can never understand or comprehend the manner nor the fashion of it, nor how nor why that touching came about. For this is the operation of God, and the source and the entry of all graces and of all gifts, and the last mean between God and the creature. And above this touching in the silent existence of the spirit there hovers an incomprehensible clarity, and that is the exalted Trinity whence this touching proceeds. There God lives and reigns in the spirit, and the spirit in God.

d. *Our response and the effect: concerning the fervent going-out of the spirit by means of a Divine touching (cap. xxi)*

Now Christ says inwardly in the spirit by means of this touching: 'Go out with exercises according to the manner of this touching', for this touching of our inmost self impels and compels our spirit to the most fervent exercise of which the creature is capable, in the manner of the creature, according to the creature's created capacity.

1. *Our response*

Here the spirit exalts itself, through its capacity for love, above works into a unity where this living spring of the touching flows. And this touching compels the understanding to acknowledge God in His clarity, and it impels and compels the capacity for love to enjoy God without any mean. And the loving spirit desires this, naturally and supernaturally, above all things. Through an enlightened reason the spirit exalts itself in a fervent contemplation, and observes and marks in the inmost part of itself, where this touching lives. Here reason and all created light fail as the spirit advances, for the Divine clarity, hovering above, which is engendered by the touching, when it encounters them dispels all created images, because it is unfathomable. And here all created understanding behaves as does the eye of the bat in the brilliance of the sunlight. Yet the spirit is ever and anew impelled and stirred, by God and by itself, to fathom these depths in which it is touched, and to know what God and what this touching may be. And the enlightened reason is ever and anew asking whence this comes, and plunging deep to track to its source this spring of ineffable sweetness. But the reason shall never be wiser concerning this than it was at the very first. And therefore reason and all observation say: 'I do not know what it is.' For the Divine clarity, hovering above, repels and blinds all understanding at their meeting. Thus God in His clarity holds Himself above all spirits in heaven and in earth. And those who have pierced with virtues and with fervent exercises down to their depths, for them this is the door of eternal life, for they are sensible of this touching. There the clarity of God shines with so great a light that reason and all understanding fail in their progress, and must falter and die before the incomprehensible clarity of God. But for the spirit which feels this in its depths, even though reason and understanding fail before the Divine clarity and remain standing outside the gates, the spirit's power of loving will still press on, for this power is impelled and compelled as is the understanding, and it is blind, and it will know enjoyment, and to enjoy is more to savour and to feel than it is to understand. Therefore love will press on where understanding is locked out.

2. *The effect*

Here begins an eternal hunger that shall never be appeased. This is an inward longing and striving of the capacity for love and of the created spirit for a good that is uncreated. And because the spirit longs to enjoy, and is impelled and spurred by God towards enjoyment, the spirit wishes always to bring this to perfection. Behold, here begins an everlasting longing and striving towards an end that is never attained. These are the poorest men on earth, for they are filled with craving and longing, for they are sick with hunger. Whatever they eat and drink, they can never be filled, for theirs is an eternal hunger. For there is no vessel ever made that can encompass the riches that are uncreate. Therefore is there this eternal hungry longing, and they are filled with God, yet never can be full. There is here great plenty of food and of drink, of which no man can know who has never felt this. But that they should be filled full in their enjoyment, that is the plenty that there they lack. And therefore their hunger is ever renewed. And yet in this touching there flow rivers honey-sweet with all delights. For this delight they savour in every manner which the spirit can think and imagine; but this is all according to the manner of the creature and beneath God, and therefore they have this everlasting hunger and impatience. Though God were to give to such a man all the gifts which all the saints have and all that man is capable of receiving, and withhold Himself alone, still the yearning desire of the soul would remain hungry and unsatisfied. God's inward touching makes us hungry and causes us to strive, for the Spirit of God drives our souls; the more He touches us, the more we hunger and strive. And these are the highest works that men perform in their life of love, above reason and understanding; for reason can neither give to love nor take from it, for our love is touched by a Divine love. And according to my understanding, there is not here nor ever shall be any separation from God. God's touching within us, so far as we can feel it, and our loving striving are both created and of the creature, and therefore they are capable of growing and increasing for as long as we live.

In this tempest of love two spirits contend, the Spirit of God and our spirit. God, by means of the Holy Ghost, inclines Himself towards us, and through this we are touched in love. And our spirit, through the operation of God and its capacity for love, hastens and inclines itself into God, and through this is God touched. From these two there rises the contention of love: there where deepest in it they meet and where it is most inwardly and piercingly visited, each spirit is wounded by love. These two spirits, that is to say our spirit and the Spirit of God, shine and illumine each the other, and each shows to the other its countenance. This constantly makes the one spirit in, love to strive after the other. Each demands of the other that which the other is, and each proffers and forces on the other that which it itself is. This makes the lover to flow away to nought. God's touching and His giving, our loving striving and our giving back to God, this holds love steadfast.

This flowing out and this flowing back again makes the well of love to overflow. In this way God's touching and our loving striving become one single love. Here man is possessed by love, so that he is able to forget himself and God, and know of nothing else but love. Thus is the spirit consumed in the fire of love, and descends so deep in the touching of God that all his striving is overpowered and all his works are ended; and his last work is that he becomes love beyond all becoming, and possesses that most innate part of his created being, above all virtue, where all works of the creature begin and end. This is the very being of love, base and foundation of all virtues. Now are our spirit and this love living and fertile in virtues. And therefore our powers cannot long endure in the unity of the spirit. For the incomprehensible clarity of God and His unfathomable love will not suffer the spirit to attain to them, and they touch the spirit's power of loving; and the spirit falls back upon its works, in a striving more exalted and more fervent than ever before. And so is the spirit more fervent and more excellent as it works its last work of working itself to nothing in love, and then it falls back again upon new works. And this is the life of heaven. And thus the ravenous spirit weens that it consumes and devours God, but the spirit remains devoured in the touching of God, and it fails in all its works, and itself becomes love above all works. For in the unity of the spirit is an uniting of the highest powers, and here are grace and love in their essence, above works, for this is the source of charity and of all virtue. Here is an everlasting flowing out in charity and in virtue, and an everlasting returning in a fervent hunger to savour God, and an everlasting abiding in a single love.

And all this is of the creature, and beneath God. And this is the most fervent exercise which one can practise in the created light of reason, in heaven and in earth; and above this there is nothing, save for a life of the contemplation of God in a Divine light and according to the manner of God. In this exercise one cannot err or be deceived, and it begins here in grace, and shall endure eternally in glory.

PART FOUR

'To meet him'. How we shall meet God spiritually, through means and without means (cap. xxii)

Now I have shown you how the man who is freely exalted through the grace of God attains to vision in inward exercises. This is, we observe, the first point that Christ demands and desires of us, when He says: 'See'. The second and the third points, where He says: 'The Bridegroom comes, go out', concerning them I have shown you three manners of the inward coming of Christ, and that the first coming has four manners, and how we shall go out with exercises according to every manner which God in His coming inspires in us, teaches us and moves us to. Now it behoves us to observe the fourth and last point, which is our meeting with Christ our Bridegroom. For all our inward seeing in grace or in glory, and all our going-out in virtue, in whatsoever exercise that may be, is all to the end of a meeting with Christ our Bridegroom and an uniting in Him, for He is our eternal rest, and the end and the reward of all our labours.

You know well that a meeting is an assembling of two persons, who come from opposite places, which in themselves are contrary and separate. Now Christ comes down from above, as a lord and a merciful giver to Whom all things are possible. And we come up from below as miserable underlings, capable in ourselves of nothing, but needing all things. Christ comes into us outward from within, and we come to Him inward from without. And therefore it is possible here for a spiritual meeting to take place. And this coming and this meeting between us and Christ is of two manners, that is, through means and without means.

A. The Foundation of all Union with God

a. *The natural union (cap. xxiii)*

Now understand and observe this carefully. The unity of our spirit preserves itself in two ways, that is essentially and operatively. You must know that the spirit in its essence receives the coming of Christ in its pure nature, without means and without interval. For the being and the life that we as images of God have, living in Him, and that we have in ourselves in our essence, they are without means and undivided. And therefore the spirit, in its most inward and its highest part, ceaselessly receives in its pure nature the impress of God's eternal image and His Divine clarity, and is an everlasting dwelling-place of God, which He possesses and eternally inhabits, and which He evermore visits with a new coming and a new enlightening by a new clarity of His eternal Nativity. For where He comes to visit, there He is; and where He is, there He comes to visit; and where He never was, there He shall never come, for in Him there is neither chance nor mutability, and all that in which He is, it is in Him, for He never goes outside Himself.

And therefore the spirit in its pure nature essentially possesses God, and God possesses the spirit, for the spirit lives in God and God with it. And the spirit in its highest part is apt to receive without any mean the clarity of God and all that God can perform. And through the clarity of His eternal image, which essentially and personally illumines it, the spirit in the highest part of its existence submerges itself in the Divine Being, and possesses there the indwelling of Its eternal blessedness, and flows out again with all creatures through the eternal Nativity of His Son, and is established in its created being, through the free will of the Holy Trinity. And here the spirit remains, like to the image of the exalted Trinity and Unity in which it was formed. And according to its created being, it receives the imprint of God's eternal image without interval, just as the flawless mirror in which the image constantly remains and in which constantly and without interval the image corresponding to your figure is renewed in fresh clarity. This essential unity of our spirit with God does not consist in our spirit, but it remains in God, and it flows out from God, and it depends on God, and it returns back again to God as to its everlasting cause, and it may never separate itself from God, nor does it in this respect do so. For this unity is within us according to our pure nature. And were the creature to separate itself from God, it would fall into complete nothingness. And this unity is above time and place, and is constantly and uninterruptedly operative according as God is eternal, except only that the spirit suffers and does not actively obtain this imprint of its eternal image, in that it is like to God and yet in itself a creature made by God. This is the excellence which we by nature possess in the essential unity of our spirit, where it is naturally united by God. This makes us neither holy nor blessed, for all men have this in them, good and evil alike; but it is indeed the prime cause of all holiness and all blessedness. And this is the meeting and the union of God and of our spirit in pure nature.

b. *The supernatural union by means* (*cap. xxiv*)

Now observe this argument carefully, for if you understand well what I wish now to say to you and what I have said just now, you shall understand all the Divine truth which any creature can teach you, and far more than that. Our spirit maintains itself operatively in this same unity in another manner, and exists for itself as in its created and personal being; that is in the quality of the superior powers which it possesses. And this is the beginning and end of every work of the creature which can be performed in manner of the creature, both in natural and supernatural matters. Yet the operation of this unity is not a single operation. But all the powers of the soul, whatever their function be, possess all their powers and their potentialities in their qualities, that is in the unity of the spirit where it remains in its personal existence. In this unity the spirit is ever able to resemble God through grace and virtue, and to be unlike God through deadly sin. For since man is made in the image of God, that is, he is made for the grace of God—for grace is a light like to God, transfusing us and making us like to Him, and without this light that makes us like Him we cannot attain to supernatural union—though we are unable to lose God's image and our natural unity with God, if we lose God's likeness, which is God's grace, we shall be damned. And therefore, whenever God finds in us some aptitude to receive His grace, He wishes to give us life and make us like to Him, out of His unstinted riches and by means of His gifts. And this comes about as often as we with all our intent turn to Him. For in that same instant Christ comes to us and into us, by means and without means, that is to say by means of gifts and above all gifts. And we also come to Him and into Him by means and without means, that is to say with virtues and above all virtues. And He imprints His image and His likeness in us, that is, Himself and His gifts; and He liberates us from sin, and makes us free and like to Him Himself. And in this same work, in which God liberates us from sin, and makes us free and like to Him in charity, there the spirit submerges itself in a delectable love. And here occurs a meeting and a union which is without mean, and supernatural, in which our highest blessedness reposes. Though everything that God out of love and His unstinted riches gives to us is natural to Him, it is to us, because of our nature, accidental and supernatural. For we before were alien from God and unlike to Him, and now again we are given His likeness, and unity with Him.

c. *The supernatural union without mean (cap. xxv)*

This meeting and this unity which the loving spirit attains and possesses without mean in God may come about in our essential comprehension, though it may be utterly hidden from our understanding if it be not understood according to the manner required by our simplicity of being. In this delectable unity we shall ever rest, above ourselves and above all things. Out of this unity all gifts flow, natural and supernatural alike. And yet the loving spirit rests in this unity above all gifts. And in this there is nothing but God, and the spirit is united without mean with God. In this unity we are received by the Holy Ghost, and we receive the Holy Ghost and the Father and the Son and the Divine nature, all in one, for man cannot divide God. And the delectable inclination of the spirit, which seeks in God an incomparable rest, obtains and possesses supernaturally, in its essential nature, all that which the spirit ever received there naturally. This is common to all good men. But how that may come about remains hidden from them all their lives, if it be that they are not inward and untrammelled by any creature. In this same instant when man turns away from sin, he is received by God into His essential unity, in the highest part of man's spirit, so that he may rest in God, now and evermore. And he receives grace and the likeness of God into the possession of his powers, so that he may ever grow and increase in new virtues. As long as this likeness to God persists in charity and in virtues, the unity persists in rest, nor may it ever be lost except through deadly sin.

d. *The necessity for grace and co-operation (cap. xxvi)*

Now all holiness and all blessedness is dependent on the soul being led, through its likeness to God and through the means of grace or of glory, to rest in the essential unity. For the grace of God is the path on which we must always advance, if we are to come into that state of naked being in which God gives Himself, in all His riches, without mean. And this is why sinners and damned spirits are in darkness, because they lack grace of God which should light and guide and lead them to the delectable unity. And yet the essential being of the spirit is so excellent that the damned cannot desire that they should perish utterly, but it is sin which forms the mean, and causes darkness, and brings about a dissimilarity to that power and that existence in which God dwells so great that the spirit in its own being cannot achieve unity; for sin deprives him of that which was his own and was to be his eternal rest. For whoever lives without sin lives in the likeness of God and in grace, and God is his own. And thus there is need of grace, which drives out sin and makes ready the way and fructifies all our life. And therefore Christ comes ever into us by means, as by graces and manifold gifts. And we too go to Him by means, as by virtues and exercises of many kinds. And as He gives to us more inwardly and moves us more subtly, so our spirit knows more inward and more joyous exercises, as you have indeed heard in all the manners which have already been shown. And this is a constant renewing. For God ever gives new gifts, and our spirit turns ever inward, according to the manners in which it is impelled and enriched by God, and in this meeting the spirit ever receives an exalted and a new enrichment in grace. And thus men ever grow in an exalted life. And this operative meeting is all through means. For the gifts of God, and our virtues, and that our spirits are operable, all these make the means. And all men and all spirits have need of such means, for without the means of the grace of God and of a loving and free conversion, no man shall be saved.

e. *How God in two-fold manner comes to meet us and demands that we go to meet Him (cap. xxvii)*

Now God beholds the dwelling-place and the rest which He has made with us and in us, which is our unity and our likeness to Him. And He wishes to visit our unity constantly with the new coming of His exalted Nativity and with the riches that flow from His unfathomable love, for He will dwell in delight within the loving spirit; and He wishes to visit our spirit's likeness to Him with rich gifts, so that in virtues we may be yet more like to Him and more illumined. Now Christ wishes that we shall dwell and remain in the essential unity of our spirit, rich with Him above all the works of the creature and above all virtue; and that operatively we shall remain in the same unity, enriched and fulfilled with virtues and with heavenly gifts. And He wishes that we shall visit our unity and our likeness to God constantly with every work that we perform. For in every renewal, God is born within us. And out of this exalted Nativity, the Holy Ghost flows with all His gifts. Now we should go out to meet the gifts of God with our likeness to Him, to meet the exalted Nativity in unity with Him.

B. THE UNION WITH MEANS

a. *In every work, through a pure intention (cap. xxviii)*

Now understand how we shall in every work go out to meet God, and grow in greater likeness to Him, and possess more excellently the delectable unity. Every single good work, however small it be, which is offered up to God with love and with an honest and single intention, earns for us a greater likeness to Him and eternal life in Him. The single intention draws together our dissipated powers in unity of the spirit, and impels the spirit on its way towards God. The single intention is the end and the beginning and the adornment of all virtues. The single intention offers to God praise and honour and all virtues, and it surpasses and transcends itself and all the heavens and all things, and it finds God in the single foundation of itself. That intention is single which intends nothing but God and all things as they exist with respect to God. The single intention drives out dissimulation and duplicity, and man shall keep it and exercise it in all his works above all things. For it keeps man continually before God, clear in understanding, zealous in virtues and free from fear, both here and in the Day of Judgment. The single intention is the single eye of which Christ speaks,[1] which, He says, shall keep bright and free from sin all the body, which is all man's deeds and all his life. The single intention is the inward enlightened loving inclination of the spirit. It is the foundation of all spirituality. It has embraced faith, hope and love, for it has faith in God and is faithful to Him. It tramples nature

[1] St. Matthew vi 22.

underfoot. And it makes peace and it stills the murmurings of the spirit, and it keeps all virtues alive, and it gives peace and hope and tranquillity in God, both here and before His judgment seat.

Thus shall we dwell in the unity of our spirit in grace and in likeness, and evermore meet God by means of virtue, and offer to Him all our virtues, all our life and all our works, in single intention, and so each hour by our every deed shall our likeness to Him grow. And from this foundation of a single intention shall we pass away from ourselves and go to meet God without mean, and rest with Him upon this foundation of simplicity: and there we shall possess the inheritance which is prepared for us since all eternity.

The life of all spirits and their virtuous works consist in their likeness to God by means of a single intention; and their highest rest consists in a simplicity which is above all likeness. Yet one spirit will exceed another in virtue and in likeness to God, and will possess its own peculiar being, according to its excellence, within itself. And to each one in its peculiarity, God is sufficient. And each one in the depths of his spirit seeks God according to the measure of his love, both here and in eternity.

b. *The order of the union by means, through the seven gifts of the Holy Ghost (cap. xxix)*

Now observe the order and the grade of all virtues and of all sanctity, and that as we shall meet God in our likeness to Him, so we shall rest with Him in unity.

1. *In the active life, by the three first gifts (cap. xxx)*

I. As man lives in the fear of God in moral virtues and in exterior exercises, and is obedient and subject to Holy Church and to God's commandments, willing and ready to perform all good things with a single intention, so he is like to God through his faith and his will, which he makes to accord with God's, doing this and eschewing that in obedience to His will, and he rests in God above all likeness. For through faith and a single intention man brings to perfection the will of God, in greater degree or in less according to his likeness to Him; and through love he rests in his Beloved above all likeness.

II. And if he exercises himself well in that which he has received from God, so God gives to him the spirit of mercifulness and of mildness. As in his heart he becomes mild, gentle and merciful, so he becomes more living and more like to God. And he feels that he rests more in God, and is in his virtues wider and deeper than before, and his likeness and his rest are to him as much the more delectable as he is the more like to God.

III. And if he exercises himself well in this, with great zeal and with a single intention and with strife against that which is in opposition to these virtues, he thus obtains the third gift, which is knowledge and discretion; and so he becomes wise, knowing what he should do and what he should eschew, where he should give and whence he should take. And through his single intention and godly love, this man rests in God in unity above himself. And he possesses himself in a likeness to God, and all his works in a greater delectation. For he is obedient and subject before the Father, and wise and discreet before the Son, and mild and merciful before the Holy Ghost. And thus he bears a likeness to the Holy Trinity. And he rests in God, through love and through the singleness of his intention. And in this consists all active life. Thus shall man exercise himself with great zeal, and pursue discreetly his single intention. And he must hold himself aloof from all that is opposed to virtue, prostrating himself ever at the feet of Christ in humility, and so each hour he shall grow in virtues and in likeness to God. And if he is thus constant, he cannot go astray. Yet, following this manner, he still remains in the active life, if it be that he pursues and exercises more the distractions that may possess his heart and the multiplicity of his works than he does the cause and the reason for which the works are performed. And if in his exercises he intend more the sacraments and the symbols and the external usages than he does the causes and reasons betokened thereby, he will always remain an outward man, and will remain intent solely upon his works. And therefore, if man wishes to approach to God and to exalt his exercises and his life, he must go in from his works to their cause, and from the symbols to the truth. So he shall be the master of his works and a confessor of the truth, and shall come into an interior life.

2. *The ascent into the life of yearning for God, by way of the four last gifts (cap. xxxi)*

IV. *By the two first manners of the first coming.* And God gives to him the fourth gift, which is the spirit of strength. So is he able to triumph over joy and woe, gain and loss, the hope and the sorrow that he has in earthly things, and over every kind of mean and multiplicity. And thus man becomes free and not ensnared by any creature. When man is undistracted by any image, he is then master over himself, and lightly and without labour he becomes unified and inward, and freely and without hindrance he turns himself to God with inward devotion, with an exalted yearning, with thanks and with praise and with a single intention. So he savours all his works and all his life, interior and exterior, for he stands before the throne of the Holy Trinity, and often he receives from God inward consolation and sweetness. For he who serves at such a banquet, with thanks and with praise and with devout reverence, often drinks of the wine and savours the meats that remain and the crumbs that fall from the table of the Lord, and always he has inward peace through the singleness of his intention. If he will stand fast before God in thanks and in praise, and in a true and upright intention, the spirit of fortitude will be multiplied twofold in him. So he is submerged, but not in any bodily affection, nor in the delight he has in consolation nor in sweetness, nor in any gift of God, nor in the rest and peace of his heart, but he wishes to pass beyond all gifts and all consolation, so that he may find Him Whom he loves. So he is strong, who forsakes and triumphs over the distractions of the heart and earthly things. And he is doubly strong who conquers and leaves behind him all consolation and all heavenly gifts. Thus man passes above all creatures and possesses himself, competent and free by means of the gift of spiritual fortitude.

V. *By the two last manners of the first coming (cap. xxxii)*

So whenever no created thing is able to triumph over him or hinder him, if he then remain standing firm in his single ascending intention and in the praise of God, and seeking and intending God above all His gifts by means of this fortitude, then God gives to him the fifth gift, which is the gift of counsel. In this gift the Father touches man from within, and calls him up to His right hand among the elect in His unity. And the Son speaks spiritually to him and says: 'Follow Me to My Father: this I will not be denied.'[1] And the Holy Ghost ravishes and enkindles the heart in burning love, and from this there comes a life of tempest and inward impatience. For he who hears this counsel is hurled into the storm of love, where nothing can content him except God alone. And therefore he forsakes himself and all things, so that he may find Him in Whom he lives and with Whom all things are one. Here man must intend God solely, and must with reason constrain himself and deny altogether his own will, and unquestioningly await the unity for which he yearns until that day when God will give it to him. So the spirit of counsel works in him in twofold manner, for he has grown to man's stature, and follows the order and the counsel of God, who forsakes himself and all things and says in his unsatisfied, tempestuous, burning love: 'Thy Kingdom come'.

And he has grown still greater and follows still better the counsel of God who conquers his own will and in love denies it, and says to God in humble adoration: 'In all things be Thy will done, not mine.' When Christ our Lord drew near to the time of His Passion, He said these same words to His Father in a humble denial of Himself.[2] And to Christ these words were most full of satisfaction and of honour, to us they

[1] Cf. St. Luke xviii 22.   [2] St. Luke xxii 42.

are the most profitable, to His Father the most lovable, and to the devil they are the most shameful words that Christ ever spoke. For in this denying of His will according to His humanity, we are all saved. Thus the will of God becomes to the loving, humble man the highest joy and the greatest consolation that his spirit may experience, even were he to go down into hell, which is impossible. And here is nature most oppressed, and God most highly exalted. And man is able to receive all the gifts of God, for he has disowned himself and has denied his will and has renounced all things for ever, and therefore he neither demands nor wishes anything but that which God will give. For the will of God is all his joy; and the man who surrenders himself to love is the freest man who lives, living without care, for God can never lose that which is His own. Now observe that even though God knows all hearts, still such a man will be tempted and tried by God until he shall be able freely to deny himself; so he may become enlightened and live to the honour of God and to his own profit. And therefore God will sometimes displace him from His right hand to His left, from heaven into hell, out of all wellbeing into great misery; and it shall seem as if he were forsaken and despised by God and by all creatures. If he has already denied himself and his will in love and in joy, so that he seeks nothing for himself but God's dearest will, he shall easily deny himself in sufferings and in misery, so that then also he seeks nothing for himself, but always the honour of God. He who is willing to do great things is also willing to suffer great things; but our torments and our sufferings when we are forsaken are more excellent before God and of greater worth to Him than are great deeds in this same time of abandonment, for to suffer is more contrary to our nature than to act. And therefore the spirit is more exalted and nature is more oppressed in heavy suffering than in great deeds, though both are achieved in the selfsame love.

If man remains in this abandonment without wishing for anything else, as one who neither knows nor desires another thing, he has thus in twofold measure the spirit of this counsel, for he is satisfactory to the will and the counsel of God in his deeds and in his suffering, and in his abandonment of himself and in his humble and prostrate obedience. And nature is adorned in the highest degree, and is enabled to become spiritually enlightened.

VI. *By the second coming (cap. xxxiii)*

And therefore God gives to him the sixth gift, which is the spirit of understanding. We have already likened this gift to a fountain with three streams. For it establishes our spirit in unity, and it makes truth manifest, and it makes in us a love that is embracing and common to all men. This gift is also truly like to the shining of the sun, for the sun with its shining fills the air with a single clarity. And it illuminates all objects, and shows the difference between all colours. And by this means it demonstrates its own power, and its heat is common to all the world for its profit and fruitfulness.

So in the same way the first shining of this gift makes unity in the soul, and the unity is illuminated with a peculiar clarity, just as is the air of heaven by the light of the sun. For the grace of God, which is the one foundation of all gifts, shines into the understanding of which we by nature are capable, essentially as a single light. And by means of this single light our spirit is established, unified, illumined, filled with graces and Divine gifts. And so our spirit is like to God, by means of grace and Divine love.

And because the spirit has this likeness, and is intent solely upon God, and loves Him above all His gifts, so it will not be satisfied with any likeness or created clarity; for the spirit in all its depths is inclined naturally and supernaturally towards that unfathomable Being whence it flowed. And the unity of the Divine Being evermore draws all likeness into the same unity. And therefore the spirit is submerged in delight, and flows away into God as into its everlasting rest. For the grace of God is in relation to God as is the sun's shining in relation to the sun, and grace is the mean and the way that leads us on;

and therefore it shines singly into us, and makes us God's
fellows, that is, like to Him. And each hour our likeness to
God is submerged, and dies in God, and is made one with
God, and remains one; for charity makes us to be made one
with God, and to remain and dwell one with Him. And yet
we preserve an everlasting likeness in the light of grace or
of glory, where we actively possess ourselves in charity and
in virtue. And we preserve a unity with God above our works
in a nakedness of our spirit in the Divine light, where in rest
we possess God above all virtue. For charity must evermore
be active in our likeness to God, and unity with God shall
rest eternally in a delectable love. And this is our commerce
in love.

For in the same instant and the same hour, love is active
and rests in her Beloved. And the one is strengthened by the
other. For the higher the love, the greater the rest; and the
greater the rest, the more fervent the love. For the one lives
within the other, and whoever does not love does not rest, and
who does not rest does not love. Yet, it seems to such a good
man that he neither loves nor rests in God, and this same
seeming comes from love: so that he may yearn to love more
than he is able, it seems to him that he falls short. And in this
work he savours both love and rest, for no-one can understand
how one loves actively and rests delectably, except for the man
who has forsaken himself and is free of himself and is enlightened.

Yet all lovers are one in God and in their rest, and like to
God in the work of love; for God in His exalted nature, of
which we bear a likeness, rests in an eternal delectation
according to His essential unity, and is eternally active
according to His Trinity, and each is the perfection of the
other, for rest consists in unity and action in trinity. And so
both remain to all eternity. And therefore if man is to savour
God he must love: and if he wishes to love, he must have
savour. But if he is satisfied with other things, he shall never
be able to savour what God is. And therefore we must possess
ourselves in unity in virtues and in likeness to God, and God

above ourselves by means of love in rest and in unity. And this is the first point concerning how the man who is common to all is made steadfast.

As the air is transfused by the clarity of the sun, the beauty and the riches of all the world are displayed, and man's eyes are illumined, and he is made joyful by the manifold differences of colour. So in the same way, when we are at unity within ourselves, and the natural understanding of which we are capable is illumined and transfused by the spirit of understanding, we are able to recognize the exalted attributes which are in God and are the prime cause of all His works which flow out to us. Though all men may understand the works, and God by means of His works, yet no-one is able to understand, to his own feeling nor in reality, the attributes of the works, nor yet the manner of their foundation, unless it be by means of this gift.

For the gift teaches us to speculate, and to recognize our own excellence. And it gives us discretion in virtues and in all exercises, showing us how we should live without error according to the everlasting truth. And the man whom this gift illumines may go abroad in the spirit, and with an illumined reason observe and understand all things for what they are in heaven and in earth. And therefore he goes into heaven, and there beholds and observes together with all the saints the excellence of Him Who is his Lover; His incomprehensible exaltedness, and His unfathomable deepness; His goodness and His unspeakable mildness, and all such lovable attributes which are in God our Lover without number, and are all unfathomable in His exalted nature, for He Himself is these attributes. Then the enlightened man casts down his eyes upon himself and upon all creatures, and he observes how God in His boundless mercy has created them all and has enriched their natures in many manners. And now He wishes to endow them and to make them rich supernaturally with the gift of Himself, if they will seek and desire this. All such rational observation, and the manifold discernment it brings of God's riches, rejoices our spirit, if we through the Divine love have died to ourselves in God, and live and go only in the spirit, and savour those things which are eternal.

This gift of understanding shows to us the unity in God which we have and possess through our delectable love, a love wherein we are submerged, and the likeness to God which we have in ourselves through charity and virtue. And it gives to us a light and a clarity in which we may walk in the spirit with discernment, and may speculate and recognize God in spiritual images, and recognize ourselves and all things according to the manner and the measure of the light, and according to the will of God and the excellence of our understanding. This is the second point concerning the enlightenment of the man who has become common. According to the same measure in which the air is illumined by the clarity of the sun, the heat becomes great and common to the earth in its fruitfulness. If our reason and our understanding are thus enlightened to recognize with discernment the Divine truth, then the will, which is the capacity for loving, is warmed in a rich outflowing, common to all in its faith and its love; for this gift forms in us a love that is wide and common, by means of our recognition of the truth, which we obtain out of its clarity. For those who are most single are those most steadfast and best at peace within themselves, and they are those most deeply sunk in God, and they are the most enlightened in understanding, and the most prolific in good works, and the most common in their outflowing love. And they are distracted the least of all, because they are the most like to God. For He in His Being is simplicity, clarity in His understanding, and an outflowing and common love in His works. And as we become more like to God in these three things, so are we more united with Him. And therefore we must in our depths remain single, and observe all things with an enlightened reason, and with a common love transfuse all things; just as the sun in the heavens remains what it is, single and unchanged, even though its clarity and its heat are common to all the world.

Now understand how we shall go abroad in our common

love with an enlightened reason. The Father is the beginning of all Godhead, according to His Being and His Person. Therefore we shall in the spirit prostrate ourselves in humble reverence before the exaltedness of the Father, and so we shall possess humility, which is a foundation of all virtue. We shall fervently adore the power of the Father, that is, we shall offer to Him honour and glory, and so we shall be spiritually exalted, for He in His power creates and preserves all things out of nought. We shall give praise and thanks and perpetual service to the faith and the love of God, Who has set us free from the bonds of the devil and everlasting death, and so we shall be free. We shall proclaim and lament the blindness and ignorance of human nature before the wisdom of God, and we shall desire that all men may be enlightened and obtain recognition of the truth, so that God may be acknowledged and honoured by them. We shall entreat the mercy of God for sinners, that they may be converted and progress in virtues, so that God may be yearningly loved by them. We shall in our mildness give to all those who have need of it out of the great riches of God, so that they may all be filled full and flow back again to God, so that God may be within them all. We shall offer to the honour and the glory of the Father all the service and all the works which Christ in His humanity ever performed out of love, so that all our prayers may be heard. We shall also offer to the Father in Christ Jesus all the fervent adoration of the angels and the saints and all good men, so that we may be united with them all in the honour of God. Yet more, we shall offer to the Father all the service of Holy Church, and the exalted sacrifice of all priests, and all that we can perform and understand in the name of Christ, so that we may meet God through Christ and grow like to Him in a common love, and in our singleness pass beyond all likeness and be united with Him in an essential unity. Always we shall remain with God in unity, and with God and His saints evermore flow out in a common love, and always turn inward again with thankfulness and with praise, and in a delectable love submerge ourselves in an essential rest. This is the richest life of which I know, and through this we possess the gift of understanding.

VII. *By the third coming (cap. xxxiv)*

Now understand that in this turning inward again, the delectable unity of God is as it were a darkness and a lack of manner and an incomprehensibility. And by means of love and a single intention, the spirit turns inward again, operatively, offering up all virtue; and delectably, offering up itself above all virtue. Out of this loving scrutiny there springs the seventh gift, which is the gift of savouring wisdom, and this transfuses the singleness of our spirit, soul and body with wisdom and with spiritual savour. And through this we are touched and moved by God in the unity of our spirit. And it is the entry and the foundation of all grace and of all gifts and of all virtue. And in this touching by God, to each man his exercises and his life are of good savour, according to the power of the touching and according to the measure of his love. And this Divine stirring is the most fervent means between God and us, between rest and works, between manner and lack of manner, between time and eternity. And God causes this spiritual burning in us first of all, before all gifts: yet last of all we recognize and savour it for what it is. For as with love we have sought God in all our exercises in our innermost depths, so we feel the entry of all graces and of all the gifts of God. And we feel this touching in the uniting of our highest powers, above reason, yet not without reason, for we comprehend that we have been touched. But if we wish to know what it may be or whence it may come, then reason and all created perception fail. For when the air is illumined with the clarity of the sun, although the eyes are keen and healthy, if one wishes to trace the rays which bring this clarity and to perceive them in the course of the sun, the eyes must needs fail in their task and smart to receive the shining of the rays. So in like manner the reflection of the incomprehensible light is so great in the union of our highest powers that every work of created beings who operate by perception must needs fail. And here our operative powers must suffer the operation of God upon them, and this is the source of all gifts. For if we were able to receive God in our comprehension, He would give Himself to us without mean; but that is impossible to us, for we are too limited and too little to comprehend Him. And therefore He sends His gifts into us according to the measure of our comprehension and the excellence of our exercises. For the fruitful unity of God is above the union of our powers, and ever demands from us our likeness to God in love and in virtue. And therefore we are touched anew each hour, so that we may each hour become newer and more like to Him in virtues. And out of this new touching the spirit falls into hunger and thirst, and wishes to strive for its hunger and thirst to be appeased, and wishes to fathom all depths in the storm of love, so that it may be filled full. And from this there comes an everlasting hungry striving in an everlasting want; for all loving spirits desire and strive towards God, each according to the manner of its excellence, and as they are touched by God. Yet God remains ever uncomprehended, because we desire Him in operative manner. And therefore there remains in us an everlasting hunger and an everlasting yearning, turning inward with all the saints. And in our meeting with God, the light and the heat are so great and immeasurable that all spirits fail in their task, and melt and perish in sensible love in the unity of their spirit. And here they must suffer the inward working of God as mere created things, and in this our spirit and the grace of God and all our virtue are a sensible love without works; for our spirit has exhausted itself, and has become love itself. And in this the spirit is single, and receptive of all gifts, and apt to all virtues. And so in this depth of sensible love there lives the welling stream, which is the inward shining or the inward working of God, which every hour moves us and stimulates us, and draws us in and makes us to flow out in new works of virtue. Thus have I shown to you the foundation and the manner of all virtues.

C. The union without mean, in threefold manner
(*cap. xxxv*)

Now understand that the unmeasured inward shining of God, which is a cause of all gifts and of all virtues, that same incomprehensible light forms again and transfuses the delectable inclination of our spirit without manner, that is, with an incomprehensible light; and in this light the spirit sinks away from itself into a delectable rest, for the rest is without manner and is unfathomable. And man cannot recognize it for what it is except with himself, that is, with his rest; for since all manner of recognition and comprehension consists in manner and in measure, it cannot satisfy us, but rest becomes a perpetual unrest. And therefore this single sinking of the loving inclination of our spirit makes in us a delectable love, and delectable love is unfathomable. And the unfathomable deeps of God call out to other deeps: that is to all those who are united with the Spirit of God in delectable love. This inward calling is the overflowing of an essential clarity. And this essential clarity, set and embraced in an unfathomable love, causes us to lose ourselves and flow away from ourselves into the unknown darkness of the Divinity. And so united, and without mean one with the Spirit of God, so can we in God meet with God, and with Him and in Him livingly possess our everlasting blessedness. This most fervent life is shown in three manners.

a. *The first manner, setting us free from distractions (cap. xxxvi)*

Sometimes the fervent man turns inward, in his singleness, according to his delectable inclination, above all works and above all virtues, with a single perception of delectable love. And here he meets God without mean. And out of the unity of God there shines in him a single light, and this light reveals to him darkness, nakedness and nothing. In the darkness, he will be seized, and he will fall into a lack of manner, as it were into a trackless waste. In the nakedness he will lose his observation and perception of all things, and he will be formed again and transfused with a single clarity. In the nothing all his works will fail him, for in the working of the unfathomable love of God he will be conquered. And in the delectable inclination of his spirit he conquers God, and becomes one spirit with Him. And in this union in the Spirit of God he comes to a delectable savour, and possesses the Divine Being. And he is filled full, according to the sinking away of his self into his essential being, with the unfathomable delights and riches of God. And out of these riches there flows into the unity of his superior powers the embrace and the fullness of sensible love. And out of this fullness of sensible love there flows into the heart and the physical powers a sensible, all-pervading savour. And through this all-pervading flood man is within himself immovable, having no power over himself or his works, nor does he know or feel in his innermost depths of soul and of body anything else than a peculiar clarity that comes with a sensible well-being and a pervading savour. This is the first manner, which is free from distraction. For it sets man free from the distraction of all things, and it raises him above works and above all virtue, and it unites man with God, and makes a firm steadfastness of the most steadfast exercises which man can practise. So whenever the good man is able to find in any distraction a mean or to imagine any exercise of virtue so as to lead him to this naked ingoing, as he desires, he is impeded in this same manner; for this manner is a passing over of all things into an emptiness. Thus you have the first manner of the most fervent exercise.

b. *The second manner, of active yearning (cap. xxxvii)*

Sometimes this inward man turns himself in yearning and in action towards God, so that he may offer to God honour and worship and himself and everything of which he is capable, and so be consumed in the love of God; and in this he meets with God through means. The means is the gift of savouring wisdom, which is the foundation and source of all virtue, and which incites and compels each good man in virtues according to the measure of his love, and which sometimes touches and enkindles in love the inward man so greatly that all the gifts of God, and all that God may give, except Himself, is too little for this man and does not satisfy him, but only increases his impatience. For deep within him, where all virtues end and begin, and where he in his yearning offers all virtues to God, and where love lives, there he has an inward sensation or feeling. And because of this the hunger and thirst of love become so great that each hour he surrenders himself, and fails and exhausts himself, and perishes in love. For he hungers and thirsts to taste God. And in each perception of God, he is surrounded by God and is again freshly touched in love. So, living, he dies, and dying, he is brought to life again. And thus each hour the yearning hunger and thirst of love are renewed in him. This is the second yearning manner, where love remains in its image of God, and yearns and desires to be united with God.

This manner is more profitable and honourable to us than the first, for it is the cause of the first. For no-one can attain to rest above action if he have not first loved yearningly and actively. And therefore the grace of God and our active love may be both preventive and anterior, that is, they may be exercised both before and after. For without the works of love we may neither deserve nor obtain God, nor yet retain that which we have obtained by means of the works of love. And therefore no man can attain to an emptiness who is master of himself and who can use the customs of love. So whenever the good man sets his heart upon any gift of God or upon any creature, he is hindered in this most inward exercise; for this exercise is a hunger which nothing can satisfy except God alone.

c. *The third manner, in rest and in action (cap. xxxviii)*

Out of these two manners comes the third manner, which is an inward life in accordance with justness and due proportion.

Now understand that God comes ceaselessly to dwell in us by means and without means, and He demands of us both that we enjoy Him and that we perform works, and that the one remain unhindered by the other, and indeed be ever strengthened by the other. And thus the inward man possesses his life in these two manners, that is, in rest and in action.

And in either the inward man is whole and undivided, for he is wholly in God, where in delectation he rests, and he is wholly in himself, where actively he loves. And both are admonished and demanded of him each hour by God, the rest and the action, which he must renew. And each hour his spirit in justice desires to pay that which is demanded of it by God. And therefore in every perception of God the spirit turns within itself, in action and in delectation; and so the spirit is renewed in all virtues, and is sunk more deeply in delectable rest. For God gives in the same giving Himself and His gifts, and each time that it turns inward the spirit gives itself and all its works.

For through God's single illumination and love's delectable inclination and effluxion, the spirit is united with God, and is straightway translated into rest. And through the gifts of understanding and of savouring wisdom, he is operatively touched, and in love each hour he is illumined and enkindled. And to him is shown in the spirit and prefigured all for which man may yearn. He is hungry and thirsty, for he sees the bread of angels and the drink of heaven; in love he labours greatly, for he sees his rest; he is a pilgrim and he sees the promised land; he strives in love for victory, for he sees his crown. Consolation, peace, joy, and loveliness and riches and all that may rejoice him are shown to the enlightened reason in God without measure in spiritual images, and through this showing and the touching of God, love remains operative. For this just man has made for himself a true life in the spirit, in rest and in action, which shall always remain; but in accordance with this life, he shall pass into a higher state.

Thus man has achieved this just and due proportion, and goes towards God with fervent love in everlasting works, and goes into God with a delectable inclination in everlasting rest, and remains in God and yet goes out towards all creatures in a love that is common in virtues and in righteousness. And this is the highest form of the inward life.

All men who in the same exercise have not both rest and action have not attained this justness and due proportion. This just man cannot be hindered in his going in, for he goes into himself, in delectation and in his works. But man is like a mirror which is double, receiving images on both sides. For in his highest part man receives God with all His gifts, and in his lowest part he receives through his senses corporeal images. Now man is able to go into himself as he wishes, and to practise justice without hindrance. But man in this life is changeable. And therefore often he goes out of himself, and is sensually active without need and without the command of the enlightened reason, and falls into petty faults. But all petty faults are in the loving in-going of the righteous man just as is a drop of water in a red-hot oven. And with this I leave the inward life.

d. *Deviations from these three ways (cap. xxxix)*

Now there are some men who seem good but who live a life contrary to these three ways and to all virtues. Now let each man observe and test himself.

1. *The first deviation: a false and self-regarding emptiness (cap. xl)*

Whatever man he be that is not enlightened and drawn by God to Him, he is not touched by love, and he has neither desire and its operative impulse, nor yet a single loving inclination to a delectable rest. And therefore he cannot be united with God. For all those who live without supernatural love incline towards themselves and seek their rest in things that are alien. For all creatures are naturally inclined to rest, and therefore rest is sought by good men and by bad, in various manners.

Now observe that whenever man is empty and undistracted in his senses by images, and free and unoccupied in his highest powers, he attains rest by purely natural means. And all men can find and possess this rest in themselves by their mere nature, without the grace of God, if they are able to empty themselves of sensual images and of all action. But the loving man is not able to find his rest here, for charity and the inward touching of the grace of God will not be still. And therefore the inward man cannot long remain in himself in natural rest.

But now observe the way in which men use this natural rest. It is a sitting still, without interior or exterior exercise, in emptiness until rest be found and remain undisturbed. But rest used in this manner is not permissible, for it causes in man the blindness of ignorance and the dejection of indolence. And this rest is nothing else but an emptiness into which man sinks, forgetful of himself and God and of all things which have need of action. This rest is contrary to the supernatural rest which men possess in God, for that rest is a loving flowing-away with a single perception of incomprehensible clarity. This rest in God, which is always operatively sought with fervent desires, and is found in a delectable inclination, and in the flowing-away of love is everlastingly possessed, and as it is possessed is none the less sought, this rest is exalted above the rest of nature as high as God is exalted above all creatures.

And therefore all those men are deceived whose intention it is to sink themselves in natural rest, and who do not seek God with desire nor find Him in delectable love. For the rest which they possess consists in an emptying of themselves, to which they are inclined by nature and by habit. And in this natural rest men cannot find God. But it brings man indeed into an emptiness which heathens and Jews are able to find, and all men, however evil they may be, if they live in their sins with untroubled conscience, and are able to empty themselves of all images and all action.

In this emptiness rest is sufficient and great, and it is in itself no sin, for it is in all men by nature, if they knew how to make themselves empty. But when men wish to exercise and possess this rest without the works of virtue, then they fall into spiritual pride, and into a self-complacency from which they seldom recover. And at such times they believe themselves to have and to be that which they never achieve.

When a man possesses this rest in emptiness, and when the impulse of love seems to him to be a hindrance, so in resting he remains within himself, and lives contrary to the first manner which unites man with God; and this is a beginning of all spiritual error.

And now observe a figure of this. The angels who returned into God in love and delectation, with everything which they had received of Him, found blessedness and everlasting rest. But those who turned and inclined towards themselves and sought rest in themselves through self-complacency in the light of nature, their rest was short and illicit. And they were blinded and put away from the everlasting light, and they fell into darkness and into everlasting unrest. Thus you see the first contrary manner, which is had through rest in a false emptiness.

2. *The second deviation: an active self-seeking (cap. xli)*

Now understand that whenever man wishes to have rest in emptiness without an inward yearning impulse towards God, he makes himself apt to every error. For he is turned away from God, and is inclined towards himself through natural love, and seeks and yearns for consolation and sweetness and that which is pleasing to him. And so such a man is like a chapman. For in everything he does, a chapman is bowed down over himself, and seeks and is intent upon his profit more than on the honour of God. The man who thus lives in merely natural love always possesses himself, unhindered, with all his own attributes.

And there are such who lead a hard life, in great deeds of penance, so that they may be known and observed to be of great holiness, and may also gain a great reward. For they are inclined to all natural love, and are glad to receive honour here in this time, and a great reward in eternity.

And such men greatly exercise their own choice, and desire and pray to God for many special tokens; and they are very often deceived. For sometimes through the devil the things which they desire appear to them, and these men attribute it to their holiness, and it seems to them that they merit it all. For they are proud, and untouched and unenlightened by God, and therefore they remain within themselves. And a little consolation can greatly deceive them, for they do not know what they forgo. And sometimes they are inclined, according to their pleasure, towards the inward savour and towards the spiritual enjoyment which is natural to them. And this is called a spiritual lechery, for it is an inordinate inclination towards natural love, which is always inclined towards itself and seeks its own enjoyment in all things. These men also are always filled with spiritual pride and obstinacy, and therefore their desire and their delight is sometimes so greatly centred upon the things which they desire and which they labour to have from God, that they are often deceived, and some are possessed by the devil.

These men live all contrary to charity and to the loving going-in, where man offers up himself, with everything of which he is capable, to the honour and the love of God, man whom nothing can appease or satisfy except an incomprehensible good which God alone is. For charity is a bond of love, which embraces us and in which we forsake ourselves and are united with God, and God with us. But natural love is inclined towards itself and its enjoyment, and always remains alone. And yet in exterior works natural love is as like to charity as two hairs on one head. But their intentions are different. For the good man seeks and intends and desires always the honour of God, with a heart drawn up to Him. But in natural love man always is intent upon himself and his profit.

So whenever in contention natural love overcomes charity, man falls into four sins, which are: spiritual pride, spiritual avarice, spiritual gluttony and spiritual lechery. Thus Adam fell in Paradise, and with him all human nature. For he loved himself inordinately with a natural love, and therefore he turned himself away from God and in his pride despised God's commandment. And in his avarice he desired skill and wisdom, and in his gluttony he sought savour and delight, and through this he was stirred to lechery. But Mary was a living Paradise. She found again the grace that Adam lost, and much more than he lost, for she is the mother of love. In charity she turned herself in her works towards God, and in humility she conceived Christ, and in mildness she offered Him with all His sufferings to the Father. And she had no gluttonous savour of any consolation or of any of God's gifts. And all her life was led in purity. Whosoever follows her overcomes all that is contrary to virtue, and comes to that kingdom where she with her Son reigns eternally.

3. *The third deviation: a false passive waiting upon God (cap. xlii)*

So when man has natural rest in emptiness, and in all his actions is intent upon himself, and remains steadfast and fixed in his own attributes, he cannot be united with God, for he lives without charity, and in dissimilarity to God. And here begins the third deviation, which is the worst of all, and that is an unrighteous life, full of spiritual error and all perversity. Now observe this with attention, so that you may well understand it. The men who live thus are, as it seems to them, occupied in the contemplation of God, and they believe themselves to be the holiest men alive. Yet they live in opposition and dissimilarity to God and all saints and all good men. Now observe what I shall say, and so you shall be able to recognize them both in their words and in their works.

Through the natural rest which they feel and have in themselves in emptiness, they maintain that they are free, and united with God without mean, and that they are advanced beyond all the exercises of Holy Church, and beyond the commandments of God, and beyond the law, and beyond all the virtuous works which one can in any way practise. For this emptiness seems to them to be so great that no-one ought to hinder them with the performance of any work, however good it be, for their emptiness is of greater excellence than are all virtues. And therefore they remain in mere passivity without the performance of any work directed up towards God or down towards man, just like the instrument which is itself passive and awaits the time when its owner wishes to work. For, they say, if they did anything, God would be hindered in what He would do. And therefore they are empty of all virtue, and empty to the point where they will not thank nor praise God, and there is in them neither cognition nor love, desire nor prayer nor yearning. For according to their way of thinking, they possess everything that they might pray or yearn for. And thus they are poor in spirit, for they are without desire, and they have forsaken everything, and live without any choice of their own, for it seems to them that they have passed beyond everything into an emptiness where they possess that for the sake of which all the exercises of Holy Church are ordained and set. And thus, according to them, no-one is able to give to them or to take from them, not even God Himself; for it appears to them that they have advanced beyond all exercises and all virtues. And they have attained, they think, to a perfect passivity in which they are finished with all virtues. And they say that greater labour is needed to be finished with virtue in passivity than to attain to virtue.

And therefore they wish to be free, and obedient to no-one, not to pope nor bishop nor parish priest. Though they may feign it to the outside world, in their hearts they are submissive to no-one, neither in will nor in deed, for they believe that they are empty of all matters which Holy Church observes. And therefore they say that as long as a man strives after virtue and yearns to perform the most perfect will of God, he is still an imperfect man: for he still seeks to accumulate virtue, and knows nothing of their spiritual poverty nor of their emptiness. But according to their way of thinking they are exalted above all the orders of saints and of angels and above every reward which one can in any way deserve. And therefore they say that they can never increase in virtue, that they can never deserve a greater reward, and also that they can never sin again.

For they say that they live without will, and that they have given their spirits to God in rest and in emptiness, and that they are one with God, and have become as nothing to themselves. And therefore they may freely do whatever their bodily nature desires, for they have attained to innocency and no law is laid down for them. And therefore, if it be the case that their natures are stirred to the performance of deeds in which they may delight, and through this stirring the emptiness of their spirits be somewhat interfered with or hindered, they satisfy the desires of their nature, so that their spirits' emptiness be not hindered. And therefore they pay no attention to fasting, to abstention from servile works nor to any commandment, except for the sake of men's opinion; for in all things they live without conscience.

I hope that few such men will be found, but such as are, they are the evillest and most harmful men that live, and it is hard for them to be converted. And sometimes they are possessed by the devil, and then they are so able in his service that one cannot well win them over by argument. But one can well prove that they are deceived, according to Holy Scripture and the teachings of Christ and our Faith.

Then, too, one finds another sect of perverted men who are in such matters opposed to these first. These men also persist that they too are empty of all works, and are nothing else than an instrument with which God works what He will and how He will. And therefore they say that they live in pure passivity without works; and that the works which God works with them are more excellent and more meritorious than those which any man can perform alone by the grace of God. And therefore they say that they are men passively waiting upon God, who themselves do nothing, but God does all their deeds. And these men too say that they cannot commit sin, for God does the deeds, and they are completely passive, and all that God desires is performed through them, and otherwise nothing. These men have within themselves forsaken themselves, and are empty and without works, and live without preference of any thing. And their manner of life is indifferent and humble, and they well know how to endure and suffer in equanimity all that happens to them, for it seems to them that they are an instrument with which God works according to His will. These men in many ways and in many of their works are established in a manner like to that of good men; but in certain matters they are opposed to good men, for they maintain that the things to which they are compelled from within, whether they are like to God or unlike, still come of the Holy Ghost. And in this and in like matters they are deceived. For the Spirit of God desires not and counsels not and works not in any man things unlike to the teaching of Christ and of Christianity.

It is hard for us to recognize such men, except for the man who is enlightened and has discretion of his spirit and of the Divine truth. For some of them are very subtle, and know how to disguise and gloze their error; and also they are so obstinate and so persistent in their own way that they would die rather than cede any point upon which they insist. For they consider themselves to be the holiest and most enlightened men alive. They are in opposition to the first sect, in that they say that it is possible for them to advance and to obtain merit in virtue, and the others maintain that they cannot advance, for they have achieved a life of unity and emptiness beyond which one cannot advance and in which there is no exercise.

e. *The correction of these three deviations (cap. xliii)*

These men all live in error and the greatest evil, and they are therefore to be shunned as is the fiend of hell. But if you have well understood the teaching which I have already expounded to you in various fashions, you will know well that they are deceived, for they live contrary to God and to righteousness and to all His saints. And they are all the forerunners of Antichrist, making ready his way that leads to every unbelief; for they wish to be free of the commandments of God and of virtue, and to be empty and united with God without love and charity. And they wish to live in the contemplation of God without any loving watching for Him, and to be the holiest men that live without the works of holiness. And they say that they have rest there where they do not love. And they say that they are exalted to Him Whom they do not love or desire. And they say that they are empty of all virtue and of all compulsion, so that they may not hinder God in His working. And they indeed acknowledge that God is Creator and Lord of all creatures, and yet they do not wish to thank or praise Him: that He is eternal and mighty and powerful, and yet they say that He can neither give to them nor take from them, and that they cannot advance or obtain merit in virtue. And at times they contradict this, maintaining that they deserve a greater reward than other men, for God performs their works, and they suffer passively the working of God and are themselves worked by Him. And, as they say, in this consists the highest merit.

And this is altogether erroneous and impossible, for the working of God is in itself everlasting and immutable, and He is His only work, and nothing else is He. And in this working there is no advancement nor merit of any of His creatures, for it is nothing else but God, in Whom there is neither growth nor diminution. But His creatures have their own works through the power of God, in nature and in grace and also in glory. And as the works here end in grace, so in glory they last eternally. If it were possible, which it is not, that the creature might in working perish and become as empty as it was when it was nothing, that is, if it were that the creature might become one with God in every way as once it was, it would not be possible for the creature to merit more than it then did; and also it would be no more holy or blessed than a stone or a stock; for without the works proper to us, the loving and the acknowledgment of God, we cannot be blessed. But God would still be blessed, as He was eternally, and we should have no profit of this.

And therefore all that these men say concerning emptiness is deceit. For they wish to disguise their wickedness and their perversity, and make it seem more excellent and exalted than any virtue; and what is wickedest they wish to cloak in subtleties, so that that may seem the best. These men are opposed to God and all His saints. But they are indeed like to the damned spirits in hell. For the damned spirits are without love and acknowledgment, and they are empty of thanks and praise and of all the compulsion of love, and this is the reason why they remain eternally damned. And for these men all that is lacking is that their time should change into eternity, and then shall justice be made manifest in their works.

f. *Christ as model of union with God in rest and in action* (*cap. xliv*)

But Christ the Son of God, Who according to His humanity leads and rules all good men in the manner of their living, He was and is and evermore shall remain with all His people, that is with all the saints, loving and yearning, thanking and praising His heavenly Father. Furthermore, His soul was and is united and blessed in the Divine Being. But He never could attain to this emptiness, nor shall He ever, for His glorious soul and all the blessed possess an eternal compulsion in love, just as those who hunger and thirst and have savoured God and can never again be satisfied. Yet this very soul of Christ and all the saints have delectation in God above the measure of desire, where there is nothing but unity, which is the everlasting blessedness of God and all His elect.

And therefore the blessedness of Christ and all His saints consists in delectation and in working; and this is the life of all good men, of each according to the measure of his love. And this is a righteousness that shall never pass away. And therefore we must adorn ourselves within and without with virtues and with piety, as did the saints. And in love and in humility we must present ourselves before the eyes of God with all our works: so shall we meet God, by means of all His gifts, and then we shall be touched with a sensible love and filled full of a common faith. And so we shall flow out and flow back again in righteous charity, and we shall be established and remain steadfast in undivided peace and in a likeness to God. And by means of this likeness and a delectable love and a Divine clarity, we shall flow away from ourselves into unity, and through God we shall meet with Him without mean in delectable rest. And so we shall remain in Him eternally and shall evermore flow out and straightway turn inward again. And through this we shall possess a true inward life in all perfection. That this may come to pass in us, may God help us.

Amen.

BOOK THREE

THE LIFE OF
CONTEMPLATION OF GOD

THE inward lover of God who possesses God in delectable rest, and himself in a compelling and active love, and all his life in virtues with justness and due proportion, through these three points and the secret revelations of God the inward man attains to a life of contemplation of God; that is, the lover who is inward and just, whom God in His free will chooses and exalts to a superessential contemplation in the Divine light and according to the manner of God. This contemplation establishes us in a purity which is above all our understanding, for it is a peculiar adornment and a heavenly crown and in addition an everlasting reward for all virtue and all life. And no-one can attain to this through knowledge or skill, nor with any exercise, but only he whom God will unite with Him in spirit, and will illumine with Himself, is able to contemplate God, and no-one else.

The secret nature of the Divinity, as it has the manner of the Persons, is everlastingly active in contemplation and love, and is everlastingly in delectation in the uniting of the Persons in the unity of Their essence. In this uniting in the essential unity of God all inward spirits are one with God in a loving flowing-out, and they are one in themselves, that same oneness that the Divine essence itself is, as they have the manner of blessedness. And in this high unity of the Divine natures, the heavenly Father is a source and a beginning of all the works that are worked in heaven and in earth. And He says in the hidden depths of our spirit: 'See, the Bridegroom comes, go out towards Him.'

Let us now make plain and expound these words as they concern a superessential contemplation, which is the foundation of all holiness and of all the life that men can live.

There are few who can attain to this Divine contemplation, because of men's own ineptitude and inability, and because the light by which men contemplate is a hidden light. And therefore no-one shall utterly understand the depths of

179

what we now expound by means of any instruction or of any narrow observation of his own. For all words and everything which a man of his natural powers is able to learn and understand, all this is far beneath the truth which I mean, and foreign to it. But the man who is united with God and illumined by this truth, he is able, through the truth, to understand it. For to comprehend and understand God, above all use of image and analogy, as He is in Himself, that is to be God, with God, without mean or any inequality which could hinder us or make means. And therefore I desire that every man who does not in the delectable unity of his spirit understand or feel this, that he remain unperturbed and leave matters as they are. For what I wish to say is true, and Christ the everlasting Truth has Himself said it in His teachings in many places, if it were so that we could well reveal and show it. And therefore he who shall understand this must have died to himself and live in God, and he must turn his face to the eternal light in the depths of his spirit, where the secret truth reveals itself without mean.

PART ONE

'See'. The conditions for seeing (cap. i)

FOR the heavenly Father wishes that we should see, because
He is a Father of light.[1] And therefore He speaks eternally,
without mean and without ceasing, in the secret places of our
spirit, one single unfathomable word and nothing more. And
in this word He enunciates Himself and all things. And this
word is nothing else than 'See'; and this is the going-out and
the birth of the Son of everlasting light, in Whom men
recognize and see all blessedness.

A. THE NECESSARY ABILITY (*cap. ii*)

If the spirit is now with God to contemplate God without
means in this Divine light, there are three things which are
necessary to man. The first is that he must be well ordered in
all virtues from without, and that within he be unhindered,
and that he be empty of all outward works, just as though he
performed nothing. For if within he is preoccupied with any
work of virtue, so he is distracted by images. As long as this
lasts in him, he is unable to contemplate. Secondly, he must
within depend upon God with compelling intention and love,
just as a kindled and glowing fire that never again can be put
out. And when he feels himself to be thus, then he is able to
contemplate. Thirdly, he must have lost himself in a lack of
manner, and in a darkness in which all contemplative men
fare in delectation, and can never again find themselves in any
way natural to the creature.

[1] Cf. St James i 17.
181

B. THE ILLUMINING WORD (*cap. iii*)

In the depths of this darkness, in which the loving spirit has died to itself, begins the revelation of God and the eternal life. For in this darkness there shines and there is born an incomprehensible light, which is the Son of God, in Whom we contemplate eternal life. And in this light we see. And this Divine light is given in the simple being of the spirit, where the spirit receives the clarity which is God Himself, above all gifts and above all works of the creature, in the empty idleness of the spirit in which it, through delectable love, has lost itself and has received the clarity of God without mean. And the spirit becomes immediately the very clarity which it receives.

Behold how this secret clarity in which man contemplates all that he has desired, in the manner of the emptiness of the spirit, this clarity is so great that the loving contemplative sees and feels in his depths where he rests nothing except an incomprehensible light. And according to the manner of this single nakedness which embraces all things, he finds himself and feels himself to be that very light by which he sees, and nothing else.

And in this you have the first point of how one sees in the Divine light. Blessed are the eyes that see thus, for they possess the eternal life.

PART TWO

'The Bridegroom Comes'. The illumination, and its effect (cap. iv)

AFTER we have thus come to see, we may joyfully contemplate the eternal coming of our Bridegroom, and this is the second matter, of which we will now speak.

What is then this coming of our Bridegroom which is eternal? That is the new birth and a new illumination without cease. For the depths from which the clarity shines forth, and which are the clarity itself, are living and fruitful. And therefore the revelation of the eternal light is ceaselessly renewed in the hidden places of the spirit. Behold, all works of the creature and all exercises of virtue may here pass away, for here God alone is His only work in the highest excellence of the spirit. And here there is nothing else than an eternal contemplation and beholding of the light, with the light and in the light. And the coming of the Bridegroom is so swift that He is always come and is always dwelling within us with all His riches; and ceaselessly and ever and again He is coming in His own Person with new clarity, just as if He never were come before. For to be come consists in an eternal now, without time, which is constantly received in new joy and new delight.

Behold how the gladness and the joy which this Bridegroom brings in His coming are unfathomable and immeasurable, for so is He Himself. And therefore the eyes of the spirit, with which it contemplates and gazes upon its Bridegroom, are opened so wide that they never may be closed again. For this beholding and contemplating of the spirit remains eternally in the secret revelation of God, and the understanding of the spirit is opened so wide against the coming of the Bridegroom that the spirit itself becomes the wideness which it comprehends.

And so with God is God comprehended and seen, wherein lies all our blessedness. This is the second point concerning how we ceaselessly receive in our spirit the everlasting coming of our Bridegroom.

PART THREE

'Go out': our life with God, remaining in Him and flowing out from Him, when we have attained to Him, our first image (cap. v)

Now the Spirit of God says within the secret out-flowing of our spirit: 'Go out in an eternal contemplation and delectation, according to the manner of God.'

A. THE REASONS MAKING POSSIBLE THIS CO-EXISTENCE

a. *That which God by His Nature possesses is possessed by us through love (cap. vi)*

All the riches which are natural in God we possess through love in God, and God possesses them in us, through the immeasurable love which is the Holy Ghost. For in this love men savour everything for which they can yearn. And therefore through this love we die to ourselves and go forth in a loving flowing-out, in darkness, and lacking all manner. There the spirit is embraced in the Holy Trinity, eternally remaining in the superessential unity in rest and in delectation. And in this same unity, according to the manner of fruitfulness, the Father is in the Son and the Son in the Father, and all creatures are in Them both. And this is above any differentiation of Persons, for here, so far as reason is concerned, we understand the nature of Fatherhood and Sonhood in a living fruitfulness of the Divine natures.

b. *Our flowing-out in God, our first image, is cause of our being (cap. vii)*

Out of this there springs and begins an everlasting going-out and an everlasting work without beginning. For here is a beginning that has no beginning. For since the Almighty Father in the depths of His fruitfulness has perfectly comprehended Himself, the Son is the everlasting Word of the Father, proceeding forth as a Second Person in the Divinity. And through the everlasting birth, all creatures proceed forth everlastingly, before ever they have been created in time. So they have seen and acknowledged God in themselves, discreetly according to the *ratio vivens*, and with that difference which is His, not, however, a difference in every respect, for everything which is in God is God.

This everlasting going-out and this eternal life which we evermore have in God, and which we are without ourselves, this is a cause of our created being in time. And our created being depends upon the everlasting Being, and it is essentially one with that Being. And this everlasting being and life which we have and are in the eternal wisdom of God, that is like to God. For it remains eternally without differentiation in the Divine Being, and it flows out eternally, through the birth of the Son, with difference and with differentiation according to the *ratio vivens*. And through these two points our being and life are so like to God that they ceaselessly acknowledge and imagine Him in this likeness as He is in Being and in Person. For even though, as the reason is concerned, all is here discretion and difference, this likeness is still one with that same image of the Holy Trinity which is the wisdom of God, in which God contemplates Himself and all things in an eternal instant before which nothing came, after which nothing goes. With a single glance He contemplates Himself and all things; and this is the image and likeness of God, and our image and our likeness, for in this God makes the image of Himself and of all things. In this image like to God, all creatures have an everlasting life, outside themselves, as it were in their everlasting exemplar. And the Holy Trinity made us in this everlasting image and in this likeness.

B. How we attain to God, our first image, and and how in contemplation and delectation with Him we remain in Him and flow out from Him
(*cap. viii*)

And therefore God would have us go forth from ourselves in this Divine light, and supernaturally attain to this image, which is our own life, and possess it with Him, operatively and in delectation, in everlasting blessedness. For there indeed we discern that the bosom of the Father is our own deepness and source, wherein we begin our life and our being. And out of our own deepness, that is, out of the Father and out of all that lives in Him, there shines an eternal clarity, which is the birth of the Son. And in this clarity, that is in the Son, the Father and all that lives in Him is made manifest to Himself. For all that He is and all that He has He gives to the Son, except only His attribute of Fatherhood, which He Himself remains. And therefore all that lives in the Father, concealed in unity, lives in the Son, flowing out and made manifest; and evermore the simple deepness of our everlasting image remains hidden in darkness and without manner. But the unmeasured clarity which shines forth from this makes manifest that concerning God which is hidden, and gives to it a manner. And all men who are exalted above their created nature into a life of contemplation are one with this Divine clarity, and they are the clarity itself. And they behold and feel and discover themselves, by means of this Divine light: they discover that they are this same single deepness, according to the manner of their uncreated nature, whence clarity shines forth without measure in a godlike manner, and yet remains evermore without manner, according as their being within is simple and single.

And therefore men who are inward and contemplative must go out, according to the manner of contemplation, beyond reason and beyond discretion; and beyond their created nature, with an everlasting beholding in this inborn light, and so they shall become transformed, and one with this same light by which they see, and which they are. And so contemplative men attain to that everlasting image in which they are made, and they contemplate God and all things without any discretion in a single act of beholding in Divine clarity. And this is the most excellent and the most profitable contemplation to which a man can attain in this life. For in this contemplation best of all does' man remain free and master of himself, and he can increase in every meritorious form of living, each time that with love he turns inward, beyond all that men can understand. For he remains free and master of himself in inwardness and in virtue. And that beholding in the Divine light preserves him above all inwardness and above all virtue and above all merit, for it is the crown and the prize for which we strive, and which in this manner we now have and possess, for the life of contemplation is the light of heaven. But if we were set free from this our exile, then we should be more apt in our being to receive the clarity, and so should the glory of God better and more excellently shine forth upon us.

This is the manner above all manners in which man goes out in a Divine contemplation and in an everlasting beholding, and in which he is transformed and formed again in Divine clarity.

This going-out of the contemplative man is also loving. For through delectable love he passes beyond his created nature, and finds and savours the riches and the joy which are God Himself, and which cause the secret places of the spirit immediately to be transfused, when now he stands made like to the high excellence of God.

PART FOUR

'To meet Him': the loving ascent, through the Holy Ghost, to the delectation of the Godhead (cap. ix)

WHEN the inward contemplative man has thus attained his everlasting image, and in this purity, by means of the Son, possesses the bosom of the Father, he is illumined with Divine truth. And each hour he receives afresh the everlasting birth, and he goes out, according to the manner of the light, in a Divine contemplation. And from this there springs the fourth point and the last, which is a loving meeting, in which above all else our highest blessedness consists.

You shall know that the heavenly Father, as He is a living depth, has gone operatively with all that lives in Him into His Son, as into the everlasting wisdom which is He; and this same wisdom, and all that lives in it, is operatively returned again into the Father, that is into the same depths whence it proceeds. And from this meeting springs the third Person, between the Father and the Son, that is the Holy Ghost, the love of Them both, Who is one with both of Them in the same nature. And the Holy Ghost embraces and transfuses, operatively and in delectation, the Father and the Son and all that lives in Them, with so great riches and joy that concerning this all creatures must evermore be silent. For the incomprehensible miracle that lies in this love everlastingly exceeds the comprehension of all creatures. But in the spirit, above himself and one with the Spirit of God, man understands and savours this wonder without wonderment, and tastes and sees without measure as God does, the riches which are God, in the unity of the living depths where man possesses Him according to the manner of His uncreated being.

Then this most blessed meeting in us according to God's manner is ceaselessly renewed operatively. For the Father gives himself in the Son, and the Son in the Father in an everlasting delight, Each in the Other, and a loving embracing, the One of the Other. And this is renewed every hour in the bond of love. For just as the Father ceaselessly contemplates all things anew in the birth of His Son, so all things are loved anew by the Father and by the Son in the flowing-out of the Holy Ghost.

And this is the operative meeting of the Father and of the Son in which we are lovingly embraced through the Holy Ghost in eternal love.

Now this operative meeting and this loving embrace are in their depths delectable and without manner. For God's impenetrable lack of manner is so dark and so without manner that in itself it comprehends all the Divine manners, and the work and the attributes of the Persons in the rich embrace of Their essential unity; and in the abyss of God's namelessness it makes a Divine delectation. And in this there is a delectable passing-over and a flowing-away and a sinking-down into the essential nakedness, with all the Divine names and all manners and all living reason which has its image in the mirror of Divine truth: all these fall away into this simple nakedness, wanting manner and without reason. For in this unfathomable joy of simplicity, all things are embraced in a delectable blessedness, and the depths themselves remain uncomprehended, except it be in our essential unity with God. Before this all created personality must fail, and all that lives in God, for here there is nothing but an eternal resting in a delectable embrace of the flowing-out of love.

And this is in the being without manner which all inward spirits have chosen above all things. This is the dark silence in which all lovers are lost. But could we thus, as I have told, so prepare ourselves in virtues, we should then hasten to divest ourselves of this our mortal flesh, and we should launch ourselves on the waves of this blessedness, and no creature could ever call us back again.

That we in delectation may possess this essential unity, and that we may clearly contemplate Unity in Trinity, grant to us that Love which denies no prayer addressed to its Divinity.

Amen. Amen.

BIBLIOGRAPHY

The chief works consulted and quoted in introduction and text are:

A. *Werken*, the four-volume critical edition of the collected works, published by the Ruusbroec-Genootschap, Malines and Amsterdam, 1932:

Vol. I *Het Rijcke der Ghelieven* (*The Kingdom of Lovers*) and *De Gheestelike Brulocht* (*The Spiritual Espousals*), edited J. B. Poukens, S.J., and L. Reypens, S.J.

Vol. II *Van den Gheesteliken Tabernakel* (*The Spiritual Tabernacle*), edited D. A. Stracke, S.J.

Vol. III *Van den Blinckenden Steen* (*The Perfection of the Sons of God*), *Van den Vier Becoringhen* (*The Four Temptations*), *Van den Kerstenen Ghelove* (*The Christian Faith*), *Van den Seven Sloten* (*The Seven Bolts*), *Een Spieghel der Eeuwigher Salicheit* (*A Mirror of Eternal Blessedness*), *Van Seven Trappen* (*Seven Steps*), and *Dat Boeksken der Verclaringhe* (*The Little Book of Enlightenment*), edited L. Reypens, S.J., and M. Schurmans, S.J.

Vol. IV *Van den XII Beghinen* (*The Twelve Beguines*), edited J. Van Mierlo, S.J., together with the probably spurious *Van den XII Dogheden* (*The Twelve Virtues*).

Readers who wish to consult the original Dutch of the *Espousals* should be sure that they possess the list of Errata published as a separate sheet and inserted in Vol. I of this edition: this list contains many short but important additions and emendations to the text which materially affect it.

Leven, the companion volume to *Werken*, a series of biographical, textual and other studies edited by the Ruusbroec-Genootschap under the title *Jan van Ruusbroec, Leven, Werken*, Malines and Amsterdam, 1931.

B. Latin translations of the *Espousals*:

    Jordaens, Willem: *De Ornatu Spiritualium Nuptiarum*, printed Paris, 1512

    Surius, Laurenz: *De Nuptiis Spiritualibus*, reprinted Cologne, 1692

C. Other works consulted:

    d'Arcy, Martin, S.J.: *The Mind and the Heart of Love* (London, 1947)

    Gerson, Jean, *Opera Omnia*: vol. I (Antwerp, 1706)

    Hodgson, Phyllis, ed.: *The Cloud of Unknowing* (London, 1944)

    Knox, Ronald A.: *The New Testament newly translated* (London, 1947: this is the translation which I have quoted in the introduction, but not in the text, where I have literally translated Ruysbroek's Dutch without reference to any other version)

    Knox, Ronald A.: *Enthusiasm, a chapter in the history of Religion* (Oxford, 1950)

    Van Mierlo, J., S.J.: articles in *Dictionnaire d'histoire et de géographie ecclésiastiques*

    Pomerius, Henricus: *De Origine Monasterii Viridis Vallis* (in *Analecta Bollandiana*, vol IV)

    de Rougemont, Denis: *L'amour et l'occident* (translated as *Passion and Society*, London, 1940)

INDEX